The Mayan Horoscope:

Ancient Secrets of the Mayan Calendar

Olivia Stone

2023

AUTHOR:
Olivia Stone

The Mayan Horoscope: Ancient Secrets of the Mayan Calendar/Olivia Stone. – Kyiv. : OVK, 2023. – 172 p.

With help of this book, you'll gain a firm foundation of all the 20-day signs that form the core of the Mayan horoscope. This belief system suggests that each day sign represents a distinct energy or archetype, thus embodying its own traits and qualities. Get ready to learn and explore the specific and symbolic meanings behind these signs, their associated elements, and the animals or natural phenomena they symbolize. By discovering and assessing your own day sign, you can soon gain valuable insights into your personality, professional aspirations, love life, and life path.

All rights reserved.
This book in whole or part may not be reproduced without the publisher's written consent by any means or in any form, including on the Internet.

© Olivia Stone, 2023
© OVK, 2023

Contents.

Introduction 4

Chapter 1 – Where Was the Mayan Calendar Found? 7

Chapter 2 – What is the Mayan Calendar? 13

Chapter 3 – Calendar structure. 20

Chapter 4 – Secrets of the Mayan Signs. 24

Chapter 5 – World Tree (Imix). 31

Chapter 6 – Wind (IR). 37

Chapter 7 – Night (Ak`bal). 44

Chapter 8 – Grain (K`an). 51

Chapter 9 – Snake (Chikchan). 57

Chapter 10 – Scull (Cimi). 64

Chapter 11 – Deer (Manik). 71

Chapter 12 – Sunrise (Lamat). 77

Chapter 13 – Water (Muluk). 85

Chapter 14 – Dog (Ok). 92

Chapter 15 – Master (Chuen). 99

Chapter 16 – Ladder (EB). 105

Chapter 17 – Reed (B`en). 111

Chapter 18 – Jaguar (Ix). 118

Chapter 19 – Eagle (Men). 125

Chapter 20 – Vulture (Kib). 132

Chapter 21 – Earthquake (Kaban). 139

Chapter 22 – Flint (Etz`nab). 146

Chapter 23 – Thunderstorm (Kawak). 153

Chapter 24 – Lord (Ajaw). 161

Conclusion. 168

Introduction.

The date of December 21, 2012 is extremely ominous. According to the Mayan calendar, on this day, a great era ended on Earth, which the Indians call the period of the Fifth Sun and lasted 5200 years.

But where did the Indians get this unknown date – 12/21/2012? Moreover, what is their mysterious calendar, which accurately surpasses the European and, in general, all world calendars?

Only some things here are so simple. The fact is that the Maya used several calendars at once. One of the calendars was intended for agricultural work and totaled (as it should be for any agricultural calendar) 365 days. However, for the performance of sacred rituals, the Maya employed a completely different calendar from ancient times, which is usually called Tzolkin, which means "counting the Sun" or "counting days" (from the Mayan words Tsol, "count," and kin, "day," "Sun").

However, in the sacred books of the Maya, this religious Tzolkin calendar has a different name: Yok-ka-Yumil, or "The Way of Our Lord." The Mayan priests considered him the main one and, like the apple of their eye, and they cherished his secrets. Diego de Landa, whose Yucatan Manuscript is the main source of information about the life of the ancient Maya, wrote about this amazing calendar: "It was the science that they believed most of all, and which they considered the highest. Not all priests knew how to understand it."

The calendar, one of the most important symbols of the greatness of the Maya civilization, was carried through centuries of oblivion and has gained worldwide fame today.

The Mayan civilization calendar is extremely complex and, unlike modern calendars, was used to not only mark dates and determine the agricultural season but also to reflect the worldview of the ancient civilization. The Mayans did not perceive time as a sequence of minutes, hours, days, and years but considered it a reflection of the cosmic order established by the gods on Earth.

Like many other cultures of Mesoamerica, the Mayas animate space and saw in the course of time the divine will and the influence of higher powers on man's fate.

The calendar was designed not only to count time relative to the events of reality but also to establish which magical forces acted in specific periods and the influence of these forces on the course of events.

All religious rites were associated with the calendar. On the days when the gods favored man, prayers were raised for the bestowal of blessings; on unfavorable days, the priests turned to Heaven with requests for protection and patronage.

According to the date of birth, fate, illness, and death were predicted, a possible profession was determined, and a name was given. The calendar was used to calculate the most successful date for sowing and harvesting, marriage and conception of a child.

One of the oddities of this calendar is that it is based not on a year or a month but on a completely incomprehensible cycle of 260 days – mind you, not 300, but 260 days, or 20 periods of 13 days.

More precisely, this 260-day cycle results from the superimposition of two cycles – a 20-day and a 13-day cycle.

The days of the 20-day cycle have their names, which successively replace each other: first comes the day of Imix (World Tree), followed by the day of Ik (Wind), then – Ak`bal (Night), etc.

However, we suggest you read about all the designations of the Mayan calendar in this book.

Chapter 1 – Where Was the Mayan Calendar Found?

The first mention of the Mayan calendar was found in the Dresden Codex, the oldest Mayan book written in America, dating back to the 11th or 12th century. The codex was rediscovered in Dresden, Germany, hence the book's current title. It presently is in the museum of the Saxon State Library.

The book was severely damaged by water during World War II. The pages are made of amate, a ficus plant. The book is 7.9 in high, and its pages fold like an accordion. When unfolded, the codex is 12.14 ft long. It is written in Mayan hieroglyphs and refers to the original text about three or four hundred years ago, describing the local history and astronomical tables. Like all other pre-Hispanic books from Mesoamerica, the Dresden Codex consists of paper made from the pounded inner bark of a wild species of ficus (hu'un in Maya, a word that has become semantically equivalent to "book"). It was from this book that the Mayan calendar was restored, and further excavations in South America only confirmed the integrity of the code.

The Maya calendar arose from the development and rise of Mesoamerican culture, as well as from the understanding of the functioning of the stars and the complex mathematical studies that characterize the Mayan civilization.

Evidence of the existence of the Mayan calendar resides in fragments of a fresco found during excavations of the Las Pinturas pyramids in Guatemala. According to researchers, they were made between 300 and 200 BC. A figure in the form of a deer's head and the number seven were painted on the damp plaster. Scientists have no doubts that this is a calendar record – one of the days in the Mayan calendar was called "7 deer."

Important archaeological discovery

Whether the deer symbol indicates a day or a year is unimportant. The main point is that scientists managed to find the oldest surviving fresco, which suggests the reality of the calendar of an ancient civilization. Something similar to hieroglyphs with dates has been seen before, but their reliability could be better. Even if old dates are indeed indicated on them, the fresco discovered by archaeologists is older by at least 150 years.

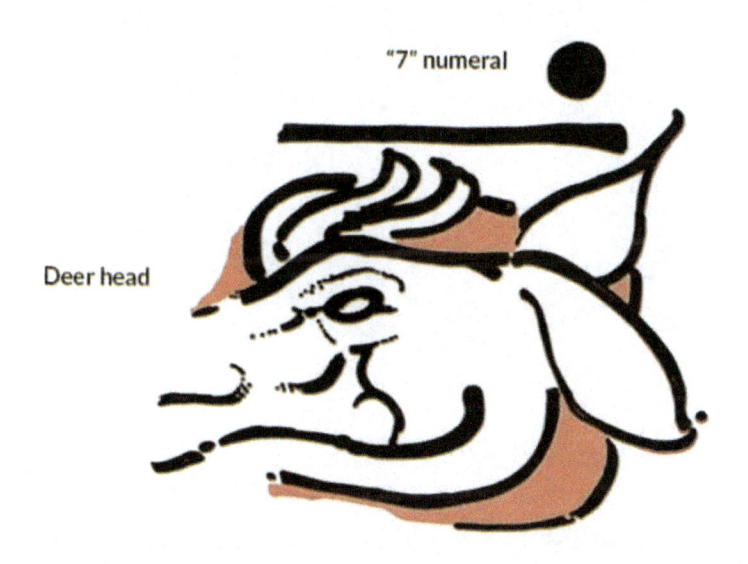

"7" numeral

Deer head

According to archaeologist Gerardo Aldana, the area of San Bartolo, where the pyramids of Las Pinturas are located, needs further research. Archaeologists may be able to make several more important discoveries that will tell even more details about the Mayan civilization and other peoples who lived next door to them simultaneously.

Mysteries of the Mayan Calendar

Probably every person imagines what the Mayan calendar looks like: it is a stone circle delineated into sectors. The calendar demonstrates a deep knowledge of astronomical cycles. It turns out that the ancient Indians calculated the almost exact duration of the solar year – 365, 242 days. Scientists believe such accurate Mayan calculations would have required about 10,000 years of constant observation. However, the period of existence of this civilization is only 3,500 years. How the ancient astronomers obtained such reliable information about the celestial cycles remains a mystery.

In addition to the two calendars mentioned above, the Indians also had a third one – the so-called "long count calendar." It was intended for large intervals of time. The duration of one complete cycle is 5125 years. The current cycle began in 3224 BC. And ended in 2012. In addition to a process of 5,000 years, the calendar mentions an even longer cycle, the duration of which is 26,000 years. Scientists attribute this period to the galactic alignment cycle.

The end of the Mayan calendar means not just the end of one cycle and the debut of another – it implies the destruction of the civilization existing in this period. The current cycle is already the fifth. The previous ones, according to the history of the Maya, ended, respectively, with earthquakes, hurricanes, volcanic eruptions, and a flood. The fifth cycle was to end with the movement of the Earth's orbit and an evolutionary leap.

Since no special catastrophes happened in 2012, either the predictions of the Mayan calendar should be considered erroneous, or the end of civilization should be understood metaphorically – as the end of a purely materialistic period in the history of humanity and the aspiration to spiritual development.

The Mayan civilization ceased to exist over a thousand years ago. The reason for it disappearance is unknown. Some historians believe that internecine wars destroyed this ancient culture; others hypothesize that natural disasters caused the death of the Maya. The indigenous people of Central America left only stone pyramids, writing, and evidence of extensive knowledge of astronomy and mathematics to their descendants.

Researchers believe that the true meaning of the Mayan calendar has to do with the natural rhythms of energy in the universe. If you consider your date of birth in the Tzolkin ritual calendar system, you can determine the name of the day and its solar seal. In Mayan chronology, each day is considered unique and has its message and purpose. You can find information on each day and try to correlate the natural rhythms of the cosmos with the events of a particular human life. The Mayan calendar allows a person to move from a purely material approach to a spiritual and intuitive one.

On the physical plane, this number system is fully consistent with the cycles of motion of large and small celestial bodies. The Indians made detailed star charts and predicted eclipses of the Sun and Moon. In addition, they knew in advance about global wars, outbreaks of worldwide terrorism, and other events that influenced the history of humanity.

Chapter 2 – What is the Mayan Calendar?

The Mayan calendar is notable for its complexity since its system consists of several calendars measuring periods of different lengths.

It is a system whose operation is explained by a set of three calendars used synchronously:
- Tzolkin: 260 days
- Haab: 365 days
- Calendar round: 52 years

The Maya used two cyclic calendars, Tzolkin and Haab, of shorter duration. In addition, they developed a long count calendar to mark dates in chronological order of historical events. Let's explore the various Mayan calendar systems and how they work below:

1. Tzolkin

It is a sacred calendar corresponding to a 260-day cycle. There are no months in this calendar, but it consists of 20 days, indicated by graphic images and glyphs, counted from 1 to 13 cyclically.

This calendar coincides with nine lunar cycles and is associated with the sun's movement, human pregnancy, the passage of the zenith, and the growth of crops.

Here is how the days were designated in this calendar:

1. Imix	2. Ik	3. Ak'bal	4. K'an	5. Chikchan
6. Cimi	7. Manik	8. Lamat	9. Muluk	10. Ok
11. Chuen	12. Eb	13. Ben	14. Ix	15. Men
16. Kib	17. Kaban	18. Etz'nab	19. Kawak	20. Ajaw

2. Haab

The Haab cycle consists of 365 days measuring the solar year. This calendar is comprised of 18 months of 20 days each, called Uinal, and a 5-day month called Wayeb, considered black days or days without a name. According to legend, it is better not to get up on these bad days because evil spirits are around.

The first day of each month was counted from 0, and this calendar marked the dates of the ceremonies and the religious calendar of the entire community.

Each month has a different name, namely:
- Pop – "mat" (July 16 – August 4)
- In – "Frog" (August 5 – 24)
- Sip – "the name of the God of the hunt" (August 25 – September 13)
- Sots – "bat" (September 14 – October 3)
- Sek – "Scull. Sermon. Bee "(October 4 – 23)
- Shul – "End. End. Dog "(October 24 – November 12)
- Yashk'in – "New Sun" (November 13 – December 2)
- Moth – "Collect. Pick up. Water" (December 3 – 22)
- Ch'en – "Well. Cave. Black "(December 23 – January 11)
- Yash – "New. Green" (January 12 – 31)
- Sak – "White, Clean. Magnificent "(February 1 – 20)
- Keh – "Deer. Forest" (February 21 – March 12)
- Poppy – "The Cover" (March 13 – April 1)
- K'an-K'in – "Yellow, Ripe Sun" (April 2 – 21),
- Muan – "Owl. Bird. Muan (April 22 – May 11)
- Pash – "Drum. Music" (May 12 – 31)
- Q'ayab – "Turtle" (June 1 – 20)
- Kumhu – "Dragon in the Cave" (June 21 – July 10)

Wayeb (July 11 – 15) had five additional "no name" days. However, these days were considered holidays since, at this time, the Maya revered some of the deities, which was the patron of the coming year.

The Mayans say that the Tzolkin without a Haab is like a soul without a body.

Here is how the days were designated in this cal-

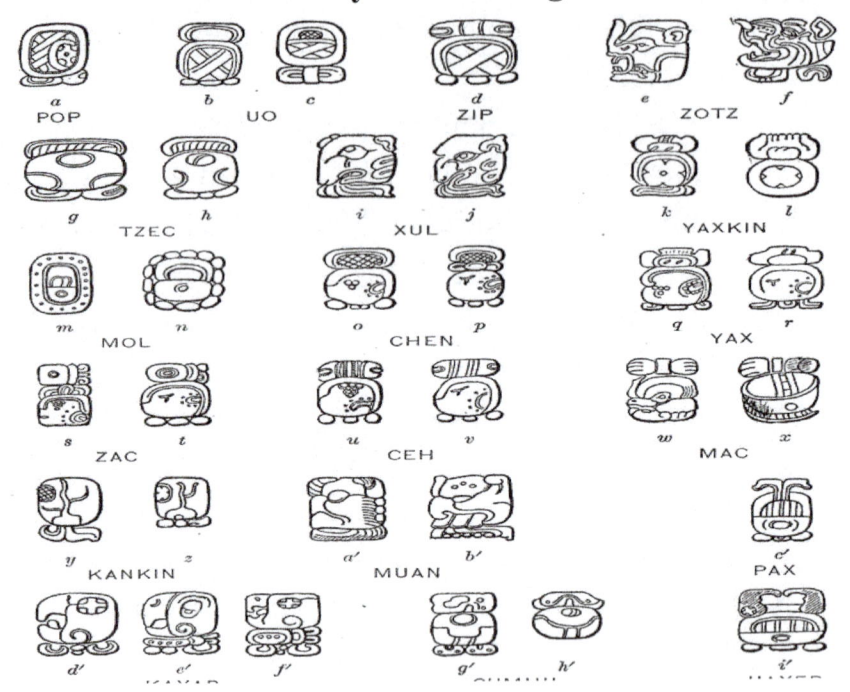

a POP, *b* UO, *c*, *d* ZIP, *e*, *f* ZOTZ

g TZEC, *h*, *i* XUL, *j*, *k* YAXKIN, *l*

m MOL, *n*, *o* CHEN, *p*, *q* YAX, *r*

s ZAC, *t*, *u* CEH, *v*, *w* MAC, *x*

y KANKIN, *z*, *a'* MUAN, *b'*, *c'* PAX

d', *e'*, *f'*, *g'*, *h'*, *i'*

endar:

Calendar round

This is the result of a combination of the 260-day Tzolkin system and the Haab system. The two calendars are combined as the names and days of the Tzolkin, resulting in 18,980 unique days, which take a total of 52 years to complete.

This is one of the most important cycles and interprets the sequence of 52-year periods marked by the New Fire ceremony, so each of these cycles was equivalent to 52 Haab circles and 73 Tzolkin circles. ...and they were considered the equivalent of the new age.

The Maya had a name for each period corresponding to their decimal system, which was the shortest cycle. They developed a long-count calendar of approximately 1,872,000 days.

This results from adding up the smallest cycles to form the longest periods. They are distributed as follows:
- Kin or sunny day, which would be equivalent to one day
- Uinal – the equivalent of 20 days (20 kin)
- Tun – equivalent to 360 days or 1 year (18 uinals)
- Katun – equivalent to 20 years (20 tun or 360 uinals)
- Baktun – equivalent to 394 years (7200 uinaals, 400 tuns or 20 katuns)
- Pictun – equivalent to 7885 years, after which came Kalabtun (20 pictoons), Kinchilbtun (20 kalabutuns), and Alautun (20 kinchilbutuns).

The long count was not a repeating system like the rest of them. It records the days from the beginning of the calendar (11th August 3114 BC according to the Gregorian calendar).

This calendar was used to record events and historical or prominent events in the cultural and political life of the Mayans

What is the last year in the Mayan calendar?

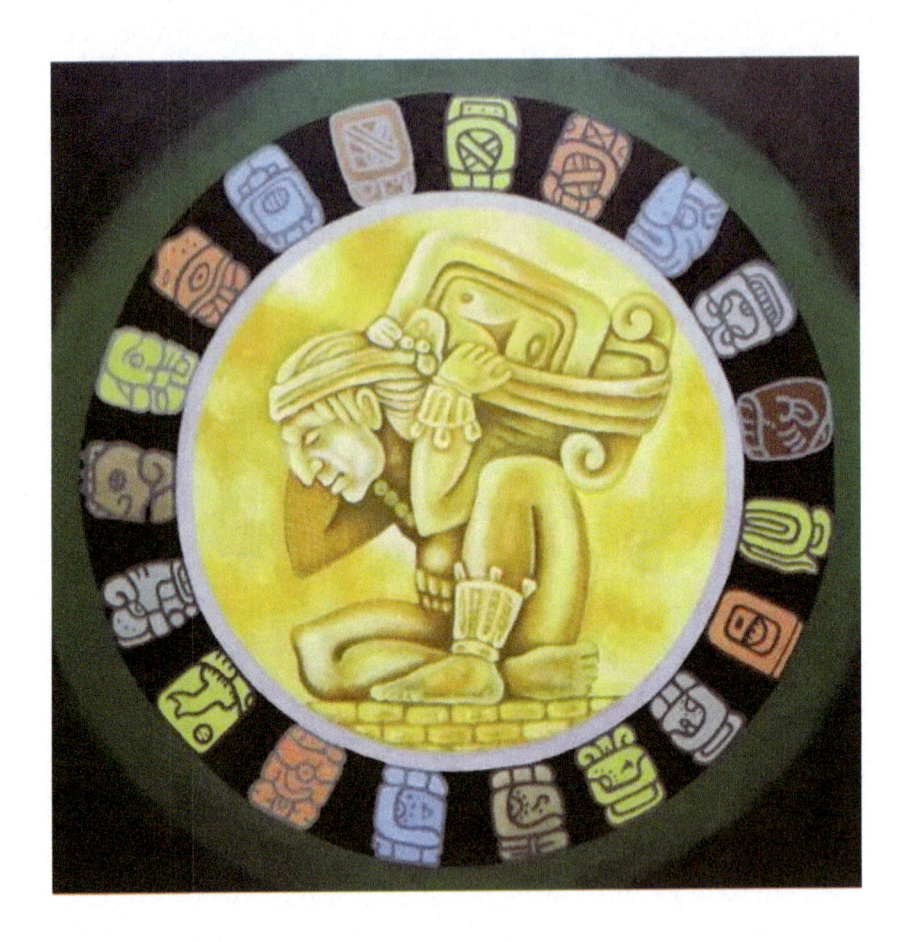

Most Mayan calendar dates result from a combination of the Tzolkin and Haab systems, forming the Calendar Wheel together. It has three wheels or circles: small, medium, and large.

The smallest circle contains 13 numbers, and the middle one consists of 20 characters or glyphs that are part of the Tzolkin system.

Then another larger wheel that serves 18 months of 20 days and a short month of 5 on the Haab system.

In some modern representations of the Mayan calendar, the three meshed wheels form a combination of 18,980 different days that return to the same point when the largest wheel completes 52 circles. To do this, the small wheel and middle wheel (Tzolkin) rotate clockwise while the large wheel rotates counterclockwise. This system serves to understand its operation. On the other hand, the Maya did not use such gears.

Time in the Mayan calendar is executed cyclically; that is, every 52 Mayan years, it starts anew. According to the accounts within the calendar itself, it began between August 1 and 11, 3114 BC, and ended on December 21, 2012 (our equivalent of the Gregorian calendar).

Chapter 3 – Calendar structure.

One of the oddities of this calendar is that it is based not on a year or a month but on a completely incomprehensible cycle of 260 days – mind you, not three hundred, but two hundred and sixty days, or 20 periods of 13 days.

More precisely, this 260-day cycle results from the superimposition of two cycles – a 20-day and a 13-day cycle.

The days of the 20-day cycle have their names, which successively replace each other: first comes the day of Imix (World Tree), followed by the day of Ik (Wind), then – Ak`bal (Night), etc. All these days are indicated in the left column of the table.

A 13-day cycle is superimposed on this cycle, the days, which do not have their names and differ only in numbers – from 1 to 13, as indicated in the table:

Name	Translation	The order of days in the calendar cycle												
Imix	World Tree	1	8	2	9	3	10	4	11	5	12	6	13	7
Ik	Wind	2	9	3	10	4	11	5	12	6	13	7	1	8
Ak`bal	Night	3	10	4	11	5	12	6	13	7	1	8	2	9
K`an	Grain	4	11	5	12	6	13	7	1	8	2	9	3	10

Chikchan	Snake	5	12	6	13	7	1	8	2	9	3	10	4	11
Cimi	Scull	6	13	7	1	8	2	9	3	10	4	11	5	12
Manik	Deer	7	1	8	2	9	3	10	4	11	5	12	6	13
Lamat	Sunrise	8	2	9	3	10	4	11	5	12	6	13	7	1
Muluk	Water	9	3	10	4	11	5	12	6	13	7	1	8	2
Ok	Dog	10	4	11	5	12	6	13	7	1	8	2	9	3
Chuen	Master	11	5	12	6	13	7	1	8	2	9	3	10	4
Eb	Ladder	12	6	13	7	1	8	2	9	3	10	4	11	5
B`en	Reed	13	7	1	8	2	9	3	10	4	11	5	12	6
Ix	Jaguar	1	8	2	9	3	10	4	11	5	12	6	13	7
Men	Eagle	2	9	3	10	4	11	5	12	6	13	7	1	8
Kib	Vulture	3	10	4	11	5	12	6	13	7	1	8	2	9
Kaban	Earthquake	4	11	5	12	6	13	7	1	8	2	9	3	10
Etz`nab	Flint	5	12	6	13	7	1	8	2	9	3	10	4	11
Kawak	Thunderstorm	6	13	7	1	8	2	9	3	10	4	11	5	12
Ajaw	Lord	7	1	8	2	9	3	10	4	11	5	12	6	13

The first day of the 260-day calendar circle, as seen in the table, is called the World Tree-1 day. Next comes Wind day-2, Night-3 day, Grain-4 day, and so on. When the number of the day reaches 13, the count is updated and starts again at one. So, for example, after the day of Reed-13, the day of Jaguar-1 follows. After 260 days, the account resumes from the beginning, that is, from the day of World Tree-1.

If a day has, a numerical value of 1, it is considered the beginning of a new 13-day cycle (the beginning of each new 13-day cycle is highlighted in blue in the table). Moreover, each cycle is called by the first day since it is the first day that leaves its mark on all 13 days of the cycle. From this, it is clear that the cycles in the Mayan calendar have the same names as the days but follow each other in a different order. First comes the World Tree cycle (beginning on World Tree-1 day), followed by the Jaguar cycle (beginning on Jaguar-1 day), then the Deer cycle (beginning on Deer-1 day), and so on.

To determine which Mayan day and cycle falls today, it is enough to know under what sign it passed yesterday. For example, if yesterday was the day Grain-3, then today, respectively, there should be Snake-4, tomorrow – Scull-5, etc.

To find out the cycle, you need to find the nearest day with the number 1 in reverse order. In the case of the Serpent-4 day, the first day of the cycle is Wind-1. Respectively, the day of Serpent-4 falls on the Wind cycle.

Traditionally, the beginning of our Maya era was chosen on the day that, according to the Gregorian calendar, falls on August 11, 3114 BC. (Thompson). This is the beginning of the Imix-5 day (World Tree-5, Earthquake cycle). Using this date as a starting point, you can determine which Mayan day and cycle falls on any date in the European calendar.

Alternatively, for convenience, in order not to be confused with the zero year (which was not in the Gregorian calendar) and other calendar subtleties, you can use any other reference point. For example: for the 20th century, it is appropriate to count from January 1, 1900 (Etz`nab – 4, or Flint-4, Eagle cycle), and for the 21st century – from January 1, 2000 (day Ik-11, or Wind-11, Stairs cycle).

This is how the Mayan calendar works in general terms. In addition to these 260-day cycles, the Maya also counted longer cycles – tuns (time intervals of 360 days), katuns (20 tuns of 360 days, i.e. 7200 days), and baktuns (20 katuns or 144,000 days). Finally, the whole era has 260 katuns among the Maya, i.e. 5200 years (more precisely 5200 tuns, corresponding to approximately 5125 solar years).

Our Mayan era is called the Fifth Sun and should end on the night of December 21, 2012. And what's next? Next is the Sixth Sun.

Chapter 4 – Secrets of the Mayan Signs.

We have so far only scratched the surface of the Mayan mysteries. The Maya didn't call their calendar "The Way of the Lord" for nothing. Indian priests believed and believed that every day the world deity, whose breath permeates all living things, undergoes certain transformations, thereby moving the evolution of living beings.

Therefore, under the sign of the World Tree, the deepest primitive instincts are activated in nature, and the sign of Wind awakens the inner Ego and self-consciousness in people. Under the sign of the Night, a person is more inclined to concentrate on his/her problems, and so on.

But the main thing is knowing the deep meaning of the Mayan signs and the order in which they follow. You can predict how events will develop on a given day or year. In other words, the Mayan calendar is a tool for a knowledgeable person to predict future events. For example, if today passes under the sign of Serpent-4, the Wind cycle, we can safely expect some unpredictable, self-willed actions from those around us.

If Herodotus had known about the Mayan culture, he would undoubtedly have attributed many of their achievements to the wonders of the world. Anyone who is at least somewhat familiar with this interesting culture is invariably surprised by two facts: firstly, their magnificent pyramids and temples, and secondly, their ancient calendar.

"This country has some secret- written in his notes Diego de Landa, who came to the Mayan country with the Spanish conquistadors, – still not solved and also inaccessible to the local people of our time.

First, these words refer to grandiose Indian buildings. As for the Mayan calendar, Landa wrote about it, how the Indians themselves considered it their main value and that not even all the priests knew how to understand its intricacies.

Indeed, the sacred Mayan calendar is a more than strange thing.

It is 105 days shorter than the usual Earth year and is not tied to the change of seasons, so using it for agricultural work is impossible. Yes, the Maya did not set themselves such a goal. They had a different calendar for agricultural work, surpassing the modern Gregorian in accuracy.

However, their main value was still considered a sacred 260-day calendar. The Europeans called this calendar Tzolkin, which in Mayan means, "counting days." The Maya themselves called it "Yok-ka-yumil," which means "The Way of our Lord" or "Footprints of God."

However, no matter what it is called, it contains information that was not known to people in the Stone Age, when this calendar was created, and until very recently.

Stone Age Medicine

We can hardly discover America if we say that in the Stone Age, there was no ultrasound, with the help of which modern doctors observe the development of the fetus in the womb. And what could the primitive Indians know about the stages of pregnancy?

Meanwhile, modern Mayan women still use their ancient calendar, claiming that it describes all the stages of the unborn child's development. We started deciphering the Mayan calendar by trying to test this claim. Indeed, the hieroglyphs and the names of some 13-day cycles themselves directly indicated the connection of the calendar with pregnancy.

Therefore, the calendar opens with a 13-day cycle with the name Imix, and its hieroglyph symbolically depicts the nipple of the female breast. The next Mayan thirteen days – Ix – means "jaguar skin." If we compare these two cycles with pregnancy, the first two weeks after conception, a woman's breasts swell, and then many pigment spots appear on the skin, similar to the spotted pattern of a jaguar.

In the same way, the Mayan cycle of Chikchan, which means "clear sign", falls just at that period of pregnancy, when all women begin to feel the regular pushes of their child.

Well, everything falls into place completely if we turn to the last calendar cycle, about which the Mayan texts say, "There the Lord created seven drains of great waters." Everyone knows that childbirth begins with the departure of amniotic fluid. As for the strange number seven, if you add it to the 260 days of the calendar, you get the average duration of pregnancy, well known to modern doctors: 267 days. However, these are only obvious coincidences.

The most interesting begins if we compare the Mayan cycles with the latest data of modern medicine.

Let us turn to the third Mayan cycle – Manik. Its hieroglyph symbolically depicts an open palm. Interestingly, it is at this time that the baby forms the palms.

Furthermore, in the cycle, the Mayan hieroglyph, which depicts a Scull, the child undergoes the formation of a skeleton. And on thirteen days, which is called Reed and expresses the idea of rapid growth, the pituitary gland of the unborn child begins to produce growth hormone. And similar coincidences with the Mayan calendar were found by us for all stages of pregnancy. A logical question arises: how could the primitive people know all this? After all, the Mayan calendar was created many thousands of years ago.

Some coincidences we discovered made us take the ancient Mayan calendar as seriously as possible. In addition to comparison with pregnancy, we analyzed the characters of people born under different Mayan signs.

For this purpose, we have chosen more than a thousand famous people whose dates of birth are not in doubt. It turned out that the ancient Mayan calendar works well at this level, and the characters of people born under the same Mayan sign largely coincide.

The most striking example here is the Mayan sign Eb – Ladder, which is said in ancient texts to be the most "social" sign. The people born under it were called the "guardians of public property."

However, it cannot be said that this calendar accurately predicts people's character. Rather, we are talking about certain inclinations given to a person by nature, which he or she can realize or not. In any case, this accuracy is sufficient to conclude that the ancient Mayan calendar is indeed one of the wonders of the world, which is still impossible to explain based on modern knowledge.

Matches real history

However, the Mayan calendar is by no means limited to influencing character. On the contrary, the Indians have always said that it equally accurately describes any processes on Earth, whether a single person's life or global historical processes.

Studying this calendar, we noticed that in addition to the 260-day cycle, it also contains cycles of 260 Mayan years and twenty years, respectively. The Mayan years and twenties have the same order as the days in a 260-day cycle. Before us, no one used this calendar in this way.

In this interpretation, the Mayan epoch, which has 5200 years, is something like the Earth's pregnancy; according to the calendar logic, it should be divided into twenty 260-year cycles. It only remained to compare these Mayan cycles with periods of real history.

Here, too, several surprising coincidences awaited us. To begin with, the very history of our civilization coincides exactly with the beginning of the Mayan era of the Fifth Sun, which began in the 4th millennium BC. During this period, the first states arose in Egypt and Mesopotamia. And the coincidences don't end there. Thus, the first empire based on military force arose in Mesopotamia during the reign of Sargon, and this happened when the Mayan cycle with the speaking name Lord took place on Earth.

It is also interesting that the heyday of Antiquity falls on the Mayan cycle with the name Master, the Great Migration took place under the Mayan sign Ok, which means the Way, and the so-called Dark Ages fall on the Mayan cycle Ak`bal, which means Night, Darkness.

Today we are living in the final phase of the entire era of the Fifth Sun – in the cycle of Dawn, and, according to the Mayan texts, in the coming years, a maximum of a decade, grandiose changes await us. However, contrary to popular belief, it is not worth waiting for some end of the world during this period. First, after the Fifth Sun, the Mayan priests promise the beginning of the Sixth. Secondly, the end of an era in the ancient books of the Maya is by no means compared with death, but rather, on the contrary, with the birth of a baby or with the sunrise after a long night. Agree. This is much nicer than a stupid fairy tale about the end of the world.

Next, we will consider the main features of each sign of the Mayan calendar. They are also the signs of the Mayan horoscope, which will help you better feel the rhythms of life, determine the nature of people born under different signs, and make independent forecasts for the future.

Chapter 5 – World Tree (Imix).

Title: IMOX / Imix (Imish).
Value: Crocodile, Dragon, World tree.
Element: Earth.
Direction: Stock.
Compatibility: Snake, Boda, Earthquake, Earth.

The meaning of the Mayan symbol

Those born on March 16, March 21, April 10, April 30, May 20, June 9, June 29, July 19, August 8, August 28, September 17, October 7, October 27, November 16, December 6, December 26, January 15, February 4, and February 24 in the Mayan Zodiac are called **IMIX.** Sometimes the sign of the World Tree is also called "Crocodile", as it is called among the Aztecs. The Mayan word IMIX means "female breast": from the Mayan "im" – "breast" and "ish" – "female", but usually this word is used to refer to the World Tree, which symbolizes the birth of life and the life-giving forces of Nature. So, in the book "Chilam Balam," the beginning of the era is symbolically indicated as the growth of the Imix Tree.

The same word is a common epithet of the ceiba tree, sacred to the Maya Indians. Indian shamans for divination, endowing them with miraculous properties, usually use its seeds.

The main element of the Mayan hieroglyph Imix symbolically depicts the nipple of the female breast, and a series of vertical lines at the bottom symbolizes the beginning of growth. Sometimes these signs are placed in a frame similar to a flower, and although the frames in Mayan hieroglyphs do not carry a semantic load, nevertheless, this emphasizes the general meaning of this sign.

In general, the sign Imix, or the World Tree, is a symbol of the beginning of beginnings, conception, and the secret source of life.

World Tree Character

A person born on the day of the World Tree feels his/her inseparable connection with the deep forces of Nature. One may not even be aware of this connection, but it is present and runs through his whole life. He/she has a very powerfully developed intuition, on which he/she used to rely more than one reason. One is in natural resonance with the surrounding world, and despite his/her often not-very-logical actions, those around him/her feel inexplicable sympathy due to his/her naturalness and organic nature. In this sense, one is like a big child with whom it is not easy but with whom it is difficult to be angry for a long time.

Indeed, the first 13 years, and especially the first year of any person's life, are under the powerful influence of this sign, so if you want to better understand the World Tree, try to imagine yourself as a baby. When a child wants to eat, drink, or something interferes with him/her, he/she does not analyze the situation but simply loudly declares his or her requirements. Of course, in an adult, under whatever sign he was born, the brain is organized much more complex. Nevertheless, the feature of putting one's desires and feelings at the forefront remains with the World Tree for Life.

When a person born on this day wants something – for example, feels sexual attraction or hunger – he/she prefers not to build complex schemes but to achieve his/her goal most simply and naturally. When he/she does not feel such desires, a force can hardly force one to do what he/she does not want.

From the outside, it often looks like a person of the World Tree quickly lights up and no less quickly loses interest in any occupation. However, this is not entirely fair. Believe me, if he/she has cooled down, it means that one has already satisfied his/her desire at the moment, but when this need arises again, one's interest will flare up with renewed vigor. In the same way, he/she is quick-tempered, but quick-tempered, because it is not in one's nature to harbor resentment for a long time.

During periods of calm and well-being, people born on the day of the World Tree are usually in harmony with the outside world and do not experience any impulses for action, being in a happy contemplative state. Nevertheless, just try to hurt them to the quick – and all their elemental power, for which there are no barriers, will immediately burst to the surface!

The fact is that the primary instincts give impetus to any of our feelings and thoughts – both the highest and the lowest, and the more powerful the primary instincts, the more difficult it is to cope with them. Try, for example, to have a leisurely small talk, it is like holding a hot frying pan with your hand! The people of the World Tree, with their most powerful instincts and emotions, experience the same thing when they have some kind of problem inside them.

On the other hand, such a force of feelings of the World Tree can find its expression in creativity, and their intuition and naturalness can only be envied.

All this shows the ambiguity of the World Tree. A person born on this day needs to learn to direct his/her enormous elemental power into some creative channel. Otherwise, it can lead him/her to no one knows where. In general, this sign is great for people of any creative profession, where not a cold mind is required, but first, intuition, depth, and naturalness of feelings.

A person of the World Tree is very susceptible to external positive and negative influences and can easily be saturated with general emotions and moods. For one's influenced, unrestrained nature, the false goods of civilization, such as drugs or alcohol, can be no small danger. An unfavorable atmosphere also greatly affects his/her mood and health, acting depressingly on him/her. Under this, a person of the World Tree can be given simple advice: to bring one's feelings into balance, he/she should often visit nature, where the world is not yet overflowing with the waste of civilization and life is as harmonious and natural as he/she is.

Man – World Tree

The male Crocodile has a strong character and always firmly follows the intended goals. If one engages in frivolous behavior in one's personal life, this person is a collected, purposeful employee in the workplace. He can change a decision abruptly and drastically, but not because of any weakness or doubts. An impulsive person is just tired of doing this business. He is attracted by new prospects. In family life, he is a loving partner, tirelessly caring for the welfare of loved ones, and gets along well with children. He devotes a lot of time to rest, especially because he likes to spend time in nature.

Woman – World Tree

The female Crocodile is an airy, unearthly creature, prefers to trust feelings and rarely considers the arguments of the mind. She is interested in everything mystical and believes in divination and predictions. She often sees priestly dreams, which one tries to follow. She rarely gets into gossip because she trusts everyone without exception. She often carelessly throws herself into the maelstrom of passions, not thinking about the consequences. She painfully experiences betrayal and deceit but still believes in true love. Needs a strong and devoted partner who will be taken care of endlessly.

World Celebrities Born on World Tree Day

- **Federico Fellini** (b. 01/20/1920) – Famous Italian screenwriter and film director.
- **Mayne Reid** (b. 04/04/1818) – English writer and author of popular adventure books.
- **Alan Alexander Milne** (b. 01/18/1882) – English writer, author of the books "Winnie the Pooh", etc.
- **Walt Disney** (b. 12/5/1901) – American animator and founder of the Disney Empire.
- **Tom Hanks** (b. 07/09/1956) – Hollywood dramatic actor.
- **Frank Sinatra** (b. 12/12/1915) – Legendary American singer.
- **Claude Monet** (b. 11/14/1840) – French painter, one of the founders of Impressionism
- **Mao Zedong** (b. 12/26/1893) – Chinese communist leader
- **Galileo Galilei** (b. 15.02.1564) – Italian scientist, one of the founders of exact natural science.
- **Alexander Bell**(b. 03/03/1847) – Inventor of the telephone.

Thomas Edison(b. 02/11/1847) – A brilliant American inventor whose name has become a symbol of invention.

Chapter 6 – Wind (IR).

Name: IQ / Ik (Iik)
Meaning: Wind, Air, Spirit, Soul
Element: Air
Direction: North
Compatibility: Wind, Scull, Dog, Jaguar, Flint

The meaning of the Mayan symbol

Those born on March 17, March 22, April 11, May 1, May 21, June 10, June 30, July 20, August 9, August 29, September 18, October 8, October 28, November 17, December 7, December 27, January 16, February 5, and February 25 in the Mayan Zodiac are called IIK (wind). The meaning of this zodiac sign is wind, air.

Mayan IK means "wind" and, like in many other ancient languages infers such concepts as Spirit, Soul, Life, and Consciousness. In the "Book of the Order of Days," it is said about this sign: "Because it was called the Wind because there was no death in it."

In general, the attitude toward the wind among the Maya Indians was ambiguous. On the one hand, the winds symbolized Nature's formidable, even destructive forces. On the other hand, the breath of life itself. Therefore, among the Mayan-Kiche Indians, the name of a single heavenly deity was Hurakan, which means "whirlwind," "tornado," and "strong wind."

The hieroglyph of the sign Wind depicts a germinating grain as a symbol of the life-giving manifestation of the spirit. It is often depicted on stone steles as a T-shaped cross.

The Mayan sign Wind – Ik – generally symbolizes the awakening of vitality and one's own "I". The wind is those primitive instincts that awaken human consciousness.

Wind character

The People of the Wind are as ambiguous as the wind itself. They have primitive unbridled energy, but at the same time, it is not a blind element but a force that is aware of itself.

The person of the Wind has a very strong consciousness, including the consciousness of his "I". His or her thought never stops. He/she rarely has a state of happy, thoughtless contemplation. On the contrary, his/her brain is always busy with something. This does not mean at all that he is constantly preoccupied with important problems – just like the rest, he/she tends to think about everything in the world, including trifles, but that's the thing that in his head, even trifling thoughts reach very significant strength. For people of other signs, such a force could acquire the character of an obsession, but for the Wind, it is a natural element to which he is accustomed and therefore knows how to cope with the powerful stream of his consciousness quite easily.

The Brain of the Wind is not the brain of a sober scientist, in whom everything is laid out on the shelves, and each thing has its own strictly defined place. His or her mind is more like an indomitable mountain stream that knows no barriers.

The main feature of the consciousness of the person of the Wind is the naturalness of his/her thinking. Although one's mind is not very organized, this is more than made up for by his/her deep intuition. He/she is not inclined to analyze the situation for too long. On the contrary, the solution to the problem suddenly comes to them, as a rule, and there is no longer any force in nature that can prevent them.

The Philosophy of the Wind is not the abstract reflection of a "scientific cracker." His/her consciousness is set in motion by life itself and therefore is inseparable from it. He/she was born in order, if not to penetrate the deep secrets of Nature, then at least to touch them.

The person of the Wind does not accept patterns that drive his thought into a rigid framework. Just as an ordinary wind cannot always blow in one direction, a person born under its sign cannot live without a feeling of freshness. That is why his/her ideas and actions fully bear the imprint of the necessary surprise and novelty.

The Force of the Wind endows a person born on this day with a very difficult character. His/her independence, tendency to authoritarianism, and peremptoriness, often bordering on intolerance, make others treat him/her with caution.

His/her behavior, like his thought, is unpredictable. It may seem to others that his interests are too diverse and replace one another too quickly, but this is an integral feature of any freethinking person. But his/her stormy energy and indomitability of consciousness can infect others with their ideas and emotions, dragging them along, a striking example of which are the incendiary dances of Michael Jackson and the irresistible smile of Adriano Celentano, born on the Day of the Wind.

The main drawback of this sign is, perhaps, that the person of the Wind does not pay attention to the possible negative consequences of one or another of his/her steps and believes in oneself and his/her strength so much that one may not notice the opinions of others. Such a feature of his is usually perceived by others as self-confidence and egocentrism – which it is. However, the Wind is not much more egocentric than the rest. Simply because of his/her powerful thinking, this trait manifests itself more noticeably and brighter. In this sense, he/she does not interfere with being more careful; remembering that sometimes, those around him/her can express sensible thoughts.

Like an indomitable consciousness, the sign of the Wind endows a person born on this day with an equally indomitable sexual temperament. His/her appetite for love can be truly impressive, but it does not mean at all that the person of Wind is doomed to inconstancy. To bring an element of novelty into his or her feelings, he/she does not have to change his partner at all. The power of the Wind's fantasy is so great that it is often enough for him/her to just play with his/her powerful imagination.

Another feature of the people of the Wind is the desire for inner freedom. Their element is space. No matter how others treat the person of the Wind, his/her inner freedom, sincerity of feelings, and brightness of thinking will never leave them indifferent. And we can say that no one will be bored next to him/her.

Man of the Wind

The charismatic man of the wind turns women's heads, not thinking about the consequences of his frivolous behavior. Sometimes too heartless and cruel, he believes that he has the right to personal freedom. He does not consider it necessary to hide his egoism and often neglects a woman's desires. Similar behavior is demonstrated at work: he is a leader who does not tolerate interference in his affairs. An extremely polite and helpful man is pleasant in communication but adamant in business matters. At the same time, he is never bored. The man of this sign is a bright personality, attracting attention with extraordinary actions.

Woman of the Wind

An imaginative woman of the wind is often captured by her fantasies. Often her picture of seeing reality differs from what is happening around her. At the same time, she considers herself a sober-minded person, capable of decisive action. In difficult situations, intuition helps her, tries to listen to her inner feelings, and acts quickly, without preliminary reflections. In her personal life, she strives to find a reliable partner. Her dream is a strong family union. But it does not leave without attention the courtship of fans, who fascinate by their lightness and immediacy.

World celebrities born on the Day of the Wind

George Lucas (b. 05/14/1944) – American director and creator of the Star Wars epic.

Al Pacino (b. 04/25/1940) – American actor.

Michael Jackson (b. 08/29/1958) – American singer, recognized king of pop music.

Whoopi Goldberg (b. 11/13/1955) – American actress, screenwriter, and TV presenter.

Snoop Dogg (b. 10/20/1971) – One of the most successful hip-hop artists in the United States.

Larry Flynt (b. 11/1/1942) – The infamous American porn mogul.

Harry Truman (b. 05/08/1884) – the 35th President of the United States, during which atomic bombs were dropped on Hiroshima and Nagasaki.

Hillary Clinton (b. 10/26/1947) – American politician.

Werner Von Braun (b. 03/23/1912) – Head of the American space program, rival of Sergei Korolev in the space race of the 60s.

Richard Feynman (b. 05/11/1918) – Outstanding American physicist, Nobel laureate.

Stanislav Lem (b. 09/12/1921) – Polish science fiction writer, author of the books "Solaris", etc.

Michael Schumacher (b. 01/3/1969) – The legendary Formula 1 racecar driver whose name has become a symbol of speed.

Chapter 7 – Night (Ak`bal).

Name: AK´AB´AL / Ak`bal (Akbal)
Meaning: Night, Darkness, Home, Sleep
Element: Water
Direction: West
Compatibility: Night, Deer, Monkey, Opel, Storm

The meaning of the Mayan symbol

Those born on March 18, March 23, April 12, May 2, May 22, June 11, July 1, July 21, August 10, August 30, September 19, October 9, October 29, November 18, December 8, December 28, January 17, February 6, and February 26 in the Mayan Zodiac are called AK`BAL.

The Mayan word Ak`bal, or Akabal, literally means "night," "darkness," and "dampness." In the Book of the Order of Days, the sign of Night has the following characteristic: "On the day of Akabal, the Lord moistened the earth, and then shaped it so that it might become a man."

The hieroglyph of this sign symbolically depicts the entrance to a cave or a hut located inside an open mouth with fangs. All this is depicted against the background of a continuous series of clouds. In the language of Mayan imagery, this expresses the idea of all-consuming darkness and solitude.

Thus, the Ak`bal sign – Night – is a sign of detachment from the outside world and focus on one's problems and experiences.

The character of the Night

The sign of the Night is amazing. The main trait distinguishing a person born on this day is his/her deep concentration on his /her problems, thoughts, feelings, and experiences. Night endows a person with such traits as strong pride, resentment, and a tendency to internal isolation, but at the same time, oddly enough, in the modern world, this sign is one of the most successful for life and career.

Therein lays its paradox. Firstly, the people of the Night have developed imagination and the ability to concentrate. Secondly, experiencing their grievances within themselves endows them with valuable qualities such as patience and perseverance.

In a word, even though the Mayan books speak of the difficult fate of the people of this sign, they also say that they are "hunters;" that is, they know how to achieve their own. Luck often accompanies them, but this happens not because of blind luck but thanks to their ability to patiently and concentrated go towards their goal.

Perhaps the most striking feature of the Man of the Night is his/her restrained independence. Unlike others, the Night rarely tries to flaunt one's independence. It's just that he/she is focused on one's own affairs and not interested in anything other than that – including the opinion of others. He/she does not like it when others climb into his/her soul, and he or she prefers not to climb into the soul of others.

This person knows how to be restrained, knows how to keep secrets, and rarely shows what true feelings lurk in his or her soul, but at the same time, one should never forget that for all his/her outward restraint, the person of the Night is very touchy. Even if he/she does not show the form, the insults in his/her soul reach a very significant strength, and he/she is not inclined to forget about them.

Externally, a person of the Night may look sociable and balanced, but no matter what impression he/she makes, he/she is always inherently closed. One is very sensitive to his/her personal space and his/her interests, putting them at the forefront of any business. Others may perceive such a feature of him/her as egocentrism, but it should be remembered that in the same way, a person of the Night knows how to respect other people's personal interests. A striking example of this is the fact that Abraham Lincoln, who gave American slaves freedom, was born on the day of the Night.

In general, the increased industriousness inherent in the person of the Night, as well as his/her ability to concentrate, can hardly be called negative qualities. It is they who help him achieve significant success in life in almost any area. As a rule, he/she pursues a goal patiently, without being distracted by trifles, watches over his/her interests, and knows how to wait. Such traits help the person of the Night in career growth, business, and creativity.

At the same time, such a feature as daydreaming is very characteristic of the people of the Night. The habit of experiencing problems within themselves gives them a developed imagination, but touchiness often gives their imagination a shade of sadness. Often it seems to them that Fate is unfair to them, that they deserve more and better, and this leaves an imprint on all their dreams and lives. In a word, the Cinderella complex in People of the Night is much more common than other signs. By the way, the brilliant storyteller Charles Perrault, who was born on the day of Night, invented the very fairy tale about Cinderella.

This, however, does not mean that the people of the Night experience more difficulties and resentments in life than others. Under their very nature, they simply experience them more deeply, which hides a considerable danger for them.

Firstly, the habit of attaching too much importance to their problems often leads to the fact that even small experiences begin to acquire the character of universal grief in their eyes. And secondly, in such a state, a person can finally withdraw into himself/herself or become hardened, blaming, if not all of humanity at once, then at least some part of it for his/her misfortunes.

It may seem strange that Nature herself provokes a person to all sorts of grief under this sign. What use can be from resentment? Meanwhile, there is a deep meaning in this: one cannot become a real human living in greenhouse conditions where everything is fine and there are no problems. The Sign of the Night is a sign test, overcoming which a person can reach great heights. No wonder they say that the stars can only be reached through thorns.

In addition, only the experience of one's own experiences can teach a person such invaluable qualities as sympathy and compassion.

One of the most striking examples of the impact of this sign is the fate of the greatest seer Michel Nostradamus. The life of this man, born under the sign of the Night, was full of hardships and trials until one day, Fate lifted him to unprecedented heights, endowing him with a prophetic gift.

Of course, not everyone born on this day becomes a prophet, but one of the features of the Night sign is that if a person passes all the tests with honor, having learned patience and sympathy, then luck will not only smile at him/her, but Nature can awaken one's amazing abilities that he/she may not even know about.

Man Night

Man Night – restrained man, who prefers to hide his real feelings and emotions. His imperturbable calmness and the ability to clearly express his thoughts give out a strong personality in him. It seems that the man is not subject to fear. He is not tormented by doubts. Surrounding people are not allowed to understand their true thoughts. He tries in vain to achieve balance, to find inner harmony. Life trials only harden his character, although he is often disappointed in people, loses interest in what is happening around him, and closes in with himself. But such behavior is rather an exception: a man of this sign is a generous, kind person who always stands up to protect weak people.

Woman Night

An insecure woman Night tends to exaggerate even the most insignificant problems. In every event, a suspicious, touchy nature looks for a catch and believes that great trials have been sent down to her. With the support of close people, she will be able to overcome inner fears, gain strength and confidence. It has all the qualities that can lead it to success: strong intuition, perseverance, and reliability. But, unfortunately, she does not find application for the abilities that nature has generously endowed her with. Too thin, this sensitive nature needs the love and care of loved ones.

World celebrities born on the day of Night

Donald Trump (b. 06/14/1946) – American billionaire.

Aristotle Onassis (b. 01/15/1906) – Greek ship-owner and billionaire.

Agatha Christie (b. 09/15/1890) – The famous English writer, a classic of the detective genre.

Jack London (b. 01/12/1876) – English classic writer, a genius of the adventure genre.

Dale Carnegie (b. 11/24/1888) – American teacher, psychologist, and writer.

Bruce Willis (b. 03/19/1955) – Cult Hollywood actor.

Jack Nicholson (b. 04/22/1937) – A cult American actor.

George Clooney (b. 05/06/1961) – A popular Hollywood film actor.

Kevin Costner (b. 01/18/1955) – American film actor.

Uma Thurman (b. 04/29/1970) – Cult Hollywood movie star.

Luc Besson (b. 03/18/1959) – Famous French film director, screenwriter, and producer.

Richard Wagner (b. 05/22/1813) – Great German composer and author of musical dramas based on mythological subjects.

Charles Darwin (b. 02/12/1809) – English scientist and creator of the theory of evolution and natural selection.

Michel Nostradamus (b. 12/14/1503) – The greatest French clairvoyant and predictor.

Chapter 8 – Grain (K`an).

Name: KAT / K`an (Kaan)
Meaning: Lizard, Grain, Iguana
Element: Fire
Direction: South
Compatibility: Lizard, Ladder, Vulture, Overlord

The meaning of the Mayan symbol

Those born on March 19, March 24, April 13, May 3, May 23, June 12, July 2, July 22, August 11, August 31, September 20, October 10, October 30, November 19, December 9, December 29, January 18, February 7, and February 27 in the Mayan Zodiac are called K`an (Grain).

"Grain" is the conventional name for this sign. Often in books about the Mayan calendar, you can also find the Aztec name for this sign – "Lizard."

Mayan K`AN means "yellow," "ripe," and "golden". The main idea embedded in the K`an sign is the idea of maturation, the symbol for the Maya is the grain. This sign symbolizes wealth in all its manifestations. It is no coincidence that the word "kan" in Indian texts is often used the meaning of "precious."

The hieroglyph of the K`an sign figuratively depicts a grain buried in the ground. Often there is also a human eye on the hieroglyph, watching the grain. This combination traces the Mayan pun: "kan" – "ripe" and "chan", "kan" – "look" (in many ancient Mayan words, the sound "h" turns into "k").

Thus, the sign K`an – Grain – expresses the idea of maturation, fertility, wealth, and future abundance.

Grain Character

In people born under the sign of the Grain, most of all, the forces and resources of the body are aimed at growth and maturation. At the body level, this means an increased activity of all physiological processes and at the level of behavior – his/her thirst for activity, a thirst for the realization of his/her ideas.

Due to this, the grain man is distinguished by increased efficiency and energy. As a rule, he does not seek to invent something completely new and original. His or her main goal is to make the most of the available resources to achieve success, and here Nature helps him/her find moves that are completely unexpected for everyone else.

Where others do not see potential, the Grain person can discover hidden resources and brilliantly realize his/her idea. Sometimes it seems that he or she, like a wizard, can create something useful literally, from nothing, getting a rabbit out of an empty hat, but this is not entirely true. It's just that his/her talent lies in bringing a living stream to those things that others may seem unpromising.

The Grain person is very observant, does not lose sight of the little things, and knows how to grasp the essence on the fly.

The main feature of the Grain person is his/her practicality and desire for concreteness; he or she does not like abstract, complex philosophies and abstract schemes. Any idea is evaluated by the Grain person, first, not through the prism of its abstract beauty but based on how effective and ultimately useful it can be. In this sense, he/she is a practitioner rather than a theorist and more of an engineer than a philosopher is.

A person of this sign is not indifferent to possessions and wealth. Moreover, Nature herself has determined that most of his thoughts and emotions are focused on this. However, this does not mean he/she is only concerned with putting his capital in a bag. On the contrary, his or her goal is to earn and spend, spend and earn, and very often, money really, as they say, sticks to his/her hands. Among the people of this sign, there are many talented business persons and simply good, highly paid workers, and although Grain people are not inclined to keep their money in their pockets idle for a long time, and even more so to stock up for the future, their energy and ability to earn money, as a rule, allow them to live on a good level.

However, this sign also has its downside. In addition to being energetic and observant, nature endowed the Grain person with a tendency to jealousy, which can manifest in him/her not only in love but also in a jealous attitude towards other people's achievements and successes. It is no secret that our world's desire for success and wealth is inevitably associated with such a concept as envy. By the very nature of the Grain man, he or she is doomed to the fact that many of those around him may experience envy of both his/her talents and abilities and his or her earnings. But he/she, for his or her part, is not devoid of this feeling; the success of others can be a very strong irritant for him/her. Of course, such feelings are familiar to everyone, but in a Grain person, they can manifest themselves with all their maximum strength, which is why he/she likes no one else, it is extremely necessary to learn how to direct this peculiarity in a positive direction. After all, the power of jealousy can always be turned with its reverse side, turning it into a healthy spirit of competition and competition.

Another feature of the Grain person is his/her tendency to excess. Often, he or she spends too many resources to achieve his/her goals and is able, as they say, to go too far. This applies to the money a Grain man can invest in his/her projects, losing all sense of proportion and to his/her health.

In other words, a person of the Grain simply needs to learn such qualities as calculation and moderation, not forgetting that his/her capabilities and the resources of his/her body, although very large, are by no means endless. They need to be replenished from time to time, giving rest not only to the body but also to the brain.

In a word, Nature showed all it's possible generosity to the people of the Grain. But to use this powerful energy with maximum benefit, they should not forget about a simple rule: everything is good only in moderation.

Man Grain

Restrained man Grain is full of secrets and mysteries. Every woman wants to know: what is hidden behind external equanimity? The secret is quite simple – a rich inner world. He is too focused on his thoughts, constantly replaying the events of bygone years in his head. He does not feel the need to clearly express his emotions and does not depend on the opinions of others at all. Painfully perceives criticism and comments but can extract a rational grain even from the most unflattering assessment of his person. Needs solitude and replenishes vitality in the bosom of nature.

Woman Grain

Woman Grain is the keeper of the hearth, disinterestedly giving her love to loved ones. She was created for the family, taking care of her relatives with pleasure. Her house is a cozy nest, a haven from the hardships of the outside world. Without regret, she sacrifices her interests for children's good and lives with their problems. Close people know that the woman Grain will give valuable advice and help resolve the most confusing situation. But with all her self-sufficiency, she needs care and longs for love and recognition of her talents. Hardly tolerates betrayal and can fall into depression.

World Celebrities Born on Grain Day

Arthur Conan Doyle (b. 05/22/1859) – The famous English writer and author of Sherlock Holmes.

Henry Kissinger (b. 05/27/1923) – American statesman and diplomat.

Elizabeth II (b. 04/21/1926) – Queen of Great Britain.

Dr. Martin Luther King, Jr. (b. 01/15/1929) – American public figure, a fighter for the rights of African Americans.

Mike Tyson (b. 06/30/1966) – The infamous American world boxing champion.

Steven Seagal (b. 04/10/1951) – Hollywood cult actor, action hero.

Jim Morrison (b. 12/8/1943) – Cult American singer, poet, and musician.

Giuseppe Verdi (b. 10.10.1813) – Great Italian composer.

Harry Houdini (b. 03/24/1874) – The great American illusionist.

Chapter 9 – Snake (Chikchan).

Name: KAAN / Chiccan (Chikchan).
Meaning: Snake, Heaven.
Element: Earth.
Direction: East
Compatibility: World Tree, Water, Reed, Thunderstorm

The meaning of the Mayan symbol

Those born on March 20, March 25, April 14, May 4, May 24, June 13, July 3, July 23, August 12, September 1, September 21, October 11, October 31, November 20, December 10, December 30, January 19, February 8, and February 28 in the Mayan Zodiac are called CHIKCHAN (Snake).

The Mayan word CHIKCHAN means "clear sign," as well as "sign of the serpent" and "Sign of the sky." The bottom line is that the ancient root "kan" (modern "kan") in the Mayan language has three equal meanings at once: "serpent," "Heaven," and "see." This ambiguity of the word "kan" explains the special love of the Indians for the image of the Serpent, which symbolically means the Divine or Highest vision.

On the hieroglyph of the Serpent sign, a mat is depicted, which in the Mayan tradition symbolizes supreme power. The mat for the Indians is the same familiar and understandable image of power as the crown or throne is for us. A special moment is connected with the fact that on the hieroglyph of the Chikchan sign, the mat is certainly located in the upper corner, which means not earthly but heavenly power. Another element of the hieroglyph is a snake, which either descends from under the mat down to the ground or, on the contrary, rises. All this symbolically depicts a certain connection between Heaven and Earth, man and God.

In general, the sign of the Snake expresses a person's connection with the higher powers.

Character Snake

The Mayan snake is one of the most beloved and respected signs. According to their observations, it is under him/her that the most powerful shamans and spirit-seers are born. Interestingly, the Bulgarian clairvoyant Vanga, whose prophetic gift was repeatedly confirmed by reputable scientists, was also born on the day of the Snake. Of course, not everyone born on this day receives such a prophetic gift. Nevertheless, there is always some special connection with the Divine in their life.

In Snake person, this special connection can be expressed in different ways, for example, in the form of extraordinary, vivid dreams or premonitions. Thanks to unconscious intuition, he/she can sometimes do things that seem illogical to others and the reason for which even he or she cannot always understand. Strange events often occur around the Snake person, it happens that life unexpectedly elevates him/her to unimaginable heights, but with the same ease, it can overthrow him/her into the very abyss.

All this is all the more unexpected because in ordinary life, the Snake, as a rule, gives the impression of a calm and balanced person, even lazy. Mayan books speak of the drowsiness that is inherent in a person of this sign, but despite this, they also say that a fire burns in his/her heart, and there are times when this fire breaks out with incredible force. In the same way, looking at a live grenade, it is not always possible to imagine what a formidable force lurks under its shell until someone pulls out the safety pin.

This is usually expressed in the fact that emotions can capture the Snake-man unexpectedly and violently, which is characteristic of him both in love and in business. Thanks to this combination of calmness and unexpectedly flashing violent feelings, the character of the Snake is very remarkable.

As a rule, the Snake person knows how to patiently and courageously endure difficult trials, but it also happens that some trifle makes him/her explode (fortunately, it does not happen so often with the Serpent). It should just be borne in mind that those things that seem like a trifle to others do not necessarily look like such in the eyes of the Snake himself or herself. No wonder the Indians compare this sign with a rattlesnake, which under normal circumstances is rather lazy, likes to bask in the sun, and never attacks unexpectedly – but just try to tickle it or pull its tail!

By nature, the Snake is very amorous. His or her feelings are distinguished by extraordinary strength and never go unnoticed. At the same time, in choosing a partner, the Snake is finicky and can hardly be satisfied with half-feelings. He/she needs true love, which captures him or her headlong and to which he/she is ready to give oneself up without a trace. When such love comes to him/her, he or she acts quickly and without looking back.

It is worth saying that the character of the Snake person is not very convenient for everyday life: it is difficult for him or her to do things that do not touch him/her to the quick. It is difficult for a snake to enter into a uniform working rhythm because he is used to acting like a jerk. It happens that he/she can work tirelessly for months, surprising everyone with his/her inexhaustible energy, and then do nothing at all for months. Even if he/she tries to adapt his impetuous nature to the conveyor, monotonous work, either the Snake itself or the conveyor will break soon.

Any profession related to creativity, whether it be literature, music, theater, or cinema, is much better suited to the Snake – here, its powerful energy can be fully used.

In any case, both the person born on this day and those around him/her should remember that the calmness and poise of the Snake are deceptive. It's just that Nature made sure that his formidable strength and mighty energy were not wasted in vain. Like a combat grenade, the purpose of the Snake person is not to methodically move towards his goal but to immediately realize his/her mighty energy at the right time and place. His or her life task is to do the impossible, thereby moving evolution forward, and in this sense, his/her drowsiness plays the role of a kind of insurance. After all, if his energy burst out continuously, it would hardly be possible to be near him/her. And the Snake person would very quickly exhaust all his/her resources.

However, in the inherent drowsiness of the Snake, there is another, very deep, meaning – it is a consequence of his/her special connection with the Higher Forces. Otherwise, it is simply impossible to touch the Divine. Even in the Bible, God says to Moses: "If there is a prophet among you, then I reveal myself to him/her in a vision, I speak to him/her in a dream" (Numbers, 12:4-8), and indeed any spiritual practices are inextricably linked with a state of trance, sleep, meditation.

In a word, we can safely say that the life of a person born on this day promises to be, though not easy, rich and vibrant. Nature ensured he or she did not become an ordinary cog in someone else's mechanism. He or she was born for more.

Male Snake

The Snake Man is a dream, an unattainable ideal. A calm, strong-willed person evokes a feeling of admiration and is always at the center of female attention. But you should not think that it is easy to win his heart. He prefers to hide his real thoughts and devotes most of his time to work. Possesses good physical health, quite seriously goes in for sports. A spiritually developed man can give a lot to his partner. She should listen to his advice and recommendations. There is no doubt that he is a reliable and worthy life partner.

Woman Snake

A bright, beautiful woman, the Snake is perfectly aware of the power of her charms. If she wishes, she can lead an idle lifestyle without denying herself pleasures. She has many talents and knows how to organize a profitable business. A hardworking and smart woman can build a successful career. She does not tolerate loneliness and passionately desires to fall in love for the last time. A romantic, sensitive person dreams of finding personal happiness. Can leave work and forget about her hobbies for the sake of her beloved man. Perhaps, more than once, she will remind you of her sacrifice in the name of the family hearth, but this is just a surge of emotions: the Snake woman was created for marriage.

World celebrities born on the day of the Snake

Oscar Wilde (b. 10/16/1854) – English classical poet.

Angelina Jolie (b. 06/04/1975) – Hollywood movie star, sex symbol.

Marilyn Monroe (b. 06/1/1926) – American superstar, sex symbol of the 60s.

Sylvester Stallone (b. 07/06/1946) – A cult American actor.

Clint Eastwood (b. 05/31/1930) – Cult Hollywood actor, director.

Charles Aznavour (b. 05/22/1924) – The legendary French singer-chansonnier.

Vanga (b. 01/31/1911) – The famous Bulgarian clairvoyant.

Christopher Columbus (b. 10/29/1451) – Great navigator and discoverer of America.

Martin Luther (b. 11/10/1483) – Figure of the Reformation in Germany, founder of the Lutheran Church.

Yasser Arafat (b. 08/24/1929) – The leader of the Palestinian people in the fight against Israel.

George W. Bush (b. 07/06/1946) – 43rd President of the United States.

Chapter 10 – Scull (Cimi).

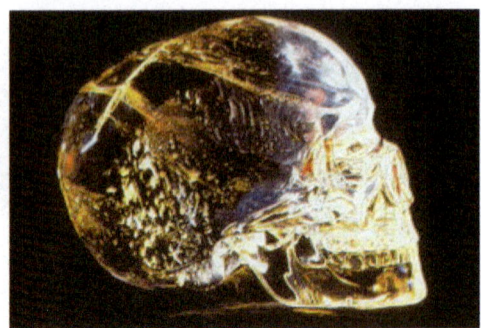

Name: KEME / Cimi (Kimi)
Meaning: Death, Scull, Wanderer
Element: Air
Direction: North
Compatibility: Scull, Dog, Jaguar, Flint, Wind

The meaning of the Mayan symbol

Those born on March 1, March 26, April 15, May 5, May 25, June 14, July 4, July 24, August 13, September 2, September 22, October 12, November 1, November 21, December 11, December 31, January 20, February 9, and February 29 in the Mayan Zodiac are called Cimi (Wanderer).

Mayan Cimi means "the one who died." However, we should not forget that the Indians had a completely different attitude toward death than the Europeans. Until now, the Day of the Dead holiday is one of the most popular in Latin America.

The Mayan sign of the Scull is a sign of testing. It symbolizes not so much death itself in our understanding of the word but such qualities of character as strength, will, firmness, and endurance. That is why, to avoid a misunderstanding of the meaning inherent in this sign, when translating, we chose one of its possible meanings – the Scull as a symbol of the strength of the human body.

The hieroglyph of the sign Cimi symbolically depicts a human scull, an indispensable attribute of which is sharp, strong teeth. A sign of power – a mat – is often inscribed inside the Scull.

Thus, the Scull is a sign of endurance and calm inner strength.

Scull character

You can often hear that the best defense is an attack, but it has absolutely nothing to do with a person born under the sign of the Scull. Nature has determined that for him/her, the best protection is calm inner firmness, caution, and restraint.

By its nature, the person of the Scull is not at all prone to aggression. Moreover, from the outside, he or she often gives the impression of a soft person, but one should never forget that he/she hides great inner strength and strong will behind this external softness, perhaps even infantilism.

If, when communicating with the person of the Scull, it seems to you that he/she is ready to give in or go against his/her inner convictions, do not be deceived by his/her calmness – he or she is not going to make any compromises, and even more so he/she is not inclined to succumb to rude pressure. Of course, like any other, the person of the Scull can temporarily retreat, but for him/her, this is by no means an admission of his or her defeat. This is just a tactic leading one to achieve one's goal. And believe me, he or she will be able to make it so that even a forced step back will eventually turn into a step toward a future victory for him/her. In this sense, the attitude of the Scull person is very similar to the ancient Chinese philosophy, which says: "The strong can defeat the weaker. The soft conquers all."

The Scull person is generally characterized by features such as the absence of rude aggression, friendliness, and outward softness, perfectly combined with his/her patience and steady desire to achieve one's goal.

The Scull person is very patient and has a considerable will. At the same time, he/she tends to act cautiously, avoiding abrupt, imprudent steps because his/her very sign calls him/his to this, gradually suggesting thoughts about the possibility of death or deadly consequences.

The Scull person knows how to wait for the right moment and is not used to rushing. That is why, from the outside, him or her often gives the impression of being slow and not even very quick, but believes me that in his/her slowness, he or she can overtake much more frisky competitors over time. By nature, he/she is more of a marathon runner than a sprinter, and he/she acts according to the well-known principle: the quieter you go, the further you will be.

However, if circumstances require a person of the Scull to act quickly, then his or her strong will can help him/her in this, although such haste is contrary to his/her nature and hardly gives him/her pleasure.

A person with this sign is also characterized by such a trait as healthy conservatism. His/her life goal is not to bring something new and original into the world but to maximally strengthen and strengthen what has already been created, using it with the greatest benefit. He/she is not inclined to retreat and change his/her beliefs. For all this, his or her behavior, as a rule, is characterized by some femininity and smoothness, which often mislead others, giving a deceptive impression of the weakness of character. The person of the Scull is a person with a strong, unbending inner core. It is simply not in his/her rules to stick out his or her inner strength for show.

When communicating with the person of the Scull, one should also consider his/her strong memory for both good and bad. Do not be deceived by his/her calmness and restraint. Believe me, he or she never forgets the insults inflicted on him/her. It does not mean that, on occasion, the person of the Scull will certainly take revenge on his/her offender. Nevertheless, he/she will always consider this fact in his/her relations with him/her.

However, not only his antipathies but also his/her sympathies (as well as his other feelings) are very constancy. Thanks to this, the person of the Scull, remembering the good, can close his/her eyes to the individual shortcomings of the other for a long time – until they reach a critical level. When it happens, you can be sure that his/her firmness will manifest itself in full here.

Nevertheless, due to its healthy conservatism, the Scull sign is favorable for a normal full life and achieving success. Due to their inner peace, people born on this day make fewer mistakes. As the great Confucius said, "The restrained have fewer mistakes," but the patience of the Scull Man helps him confidently and slowly achieve new and new heights.

Man Scull

The man of the Scull sign, possessing courteous manners, easily wins people's trust. It seems to be a soft and harmless person, but steel will is hidden behind external calmness. Acts tactfully but firmly follows the intended goals, achieving success in the chosen field. Usually, he occupies leading positions, lives in prosperity, and does not experience needs and deprivations. A woman can be sure of his honesty and decency. The man of the Scull sign is a wonderful family man: a devoted husband and a loving father.

Woman Scull

The woman of the Scull sign is full of contradictions. Her cheerful and sociable character should not be misleading. She perceives even small problems as the greatest disaster in her life. A smart, insightful woman cannot cope with her inner fears, so depression is her faithful companion. Cautiously perceives changes, and strives for a calm, measured life. But increased anxiety is just a sign of her strong intuition, a natural gift to see hidden from prying eyes. In the hands of a devoted, loving partner, she forgets about gloomy thoughts and shows her best qualities: softness, tenderness, and sincerity.

Celebrities Born on Scull Day

Bill Gates (b. 10/28/1955) – The founder of Microsoft, one of the richest people on the planet.

John Rockefeller (b. 07/08/1839) – American entrepreneur and multimillionaire, founder of the Rockefeller dynasty.

Johann Wolfgang Goethe (b. 08/28/1749) – Brilliant German classic poet and author of Faust.

Ozzy Osborne (b. December 3, 1948) – British singer and rock musician.

Jane Fonda (b. 12/21/1937) – Hollywood movie star, model, writer, and social activist.

Brigitte Bardot (b. 09/28/1934) – French film actress and fashion model, world sex symbol of the 60s.

Tom Cruise (b. 07/03/1962) – One of the richest actors in Hollywood.

Charlie Chaplin (b. 04/16/1889) – American actor and director, the genius of silent cinema.

Freddie Mercury (b. 09/05/1946) – Cult singer and vocalist of the group "Queen".

Paul McCartney (b. 06/18/1942) – A cult British rock musician, singer, composer, and one of the founders of The Beatles.

Chapter 11 – Deer (Manik).

Name: KIEJ / Manik (Manik)
Meaning: Deer, Hand
Element: Boda
Direction: West
Compatibility: Deer, Master, Opel, Storm, Night

The meaning of the Mayan symbol

Those born on March 2, March 27, April 16, May 6, May 26, June 15, July 5, July 25, August 14, September 3, September 23, October 13, November 2, November 22, December 12, 1 January, January 21, and February 10 in the Mayan Zodiac are called MANIK (Deer).

The Mayan word MANIK means "acquisition of the spirit" or "spirit of acquisition": from the root "man" – "acquire," "buy" and "ik" – "spirit, wind, desire." Among the Maya-Kiche Indians, the same sign is called the Deer, the image of which in their tradition has always been a generally understood symbol of prey. In other words, the name Deer reflects the same idea as in the word "acquisition, prey."

The hieroglyph of the Manik sign includes an image of an open palm with a circle in the middle, which symbolizes receiving something. An inverted sign is inscribed on top of the hieroglyph, meaning "spirit, wind, life," depicted as a T-shaped cross. The fact that this sign is turned upside down indicates that we are not talking about the Heavenly Spirit as such but about those desires and passions, that nature endowed a person with and that drives him/her.

Thus, the sign Deer symbolizes human desires as such, as well as the thirst for the realization of these desires.

Deer Character

In the Mayan book "Signs of the Days," it is said about the Deer: "His claws are in the blood," but if for the European ear, such an expression sounds bloodthirsty, then for the Mayans themselves, this image meant and means, first of all, prey and luck in achieving the goal.

In addition, the Maya endowed a person born under this sign with such qualities of character as pride, love of freedom, and desire for pleasures and life's blessings. The distinctive features of the Deer person are independence and the desire to live with his/her mind: he pr she knows exactly what he/she wants from life, does not tolerate interference in his/her affairs, while he or she is quite self-willed, and knows how to achieve his/her own.

Due to some hidden mechanisms of Nature, his /her clear knowledge of what he/she wants to get from life disposes of people of him/her. They begin to unconsciously go towards him/her, helping in business or making any profitable offers. Where another will have to show remarkable abilities to interest a potential partner in his/her projects, it is enough for the Deer to simply talk to him/her. It seems that Nature herself gives him/her a head start in business.

However, the Deer should consider that the unconscious sympathies of people are an advance payment, which he/she will later have to justify with his/her deeds. However, even if this does not happen, due to the same hidden mechanisms of Nature, even the obvious mistakes of the Deer rarely cause excessive irritation among others. As a rule, his/her failures end with the fact that the project is simply closed, and the Deer begins to look for a new goal for oneself.

In general, in business, the Deer relies more on intuition than logic, which helps him/her find the most advantageous place, even in unsuccessful projects. An example here is the life of an amazing person who went down in history under the name of Count Cagliostro. In some incomprehensible way, Cagliostro, born under the sign of the Deer, managed to convince others of his incredible mystical abilities. He was a member of the highest circles, talked with kings, and made his contemporaries believe in his immortality and the ability to make gold out of nothing, but, unfortunately, he ended his bright and adventurous life in an Italian prison.

All this suggests that, despite being lucky, the Deer still does not interfere with learning such necessary qualities as a sense of proportion and caution.

As a rule, Deer love to travel. They are not indifferent to beautiful things, they often arrange a festive feast with or without reason, and they can easily and recklessly plunge into a whirlpool of love adventures (although they are unlikely to forgive such ease in love to their partner). In all this, there is a considerable danger for them because, in pursuing pleasure, it is easy to lose a sense of proportion, succumbing to such eternal temptations as gluttony or alcohol.

Another pitfall of this sign is that it does not imply any morality. The personal morality of the Deer is determined by his/her desires and passions, so from childhood, he/she was not instilled with the concepts of what is possible and what is not, and what are good and what is bad. The energy of this sign can become truly dangerous – in this case, the Deer can turn into a merciless predator.

Nevertheless, the life of the Deer is determined not by any clear plan but primarily by his/her desires. Well, these desires can be very different. It's great if they find their manifestation in creative work because Deer's emotions are very contagious in the good sense of the word.

Of course, not every Deer becomes a creator, especially a genius, but all of them usually have such a trait as a love of life. Most often, this manifests in the fact that the

Deer strives primarily for the material benefits of civilization. He/she cannot be called especially greedy for money – such a trait as hoarding is alien to him/her. Money is just a means to obtain the blessings of life that the Deer needs to spend with maximum pleasure.

In other words, generous Nature provided the Deer with great opportunities to receive life's blessings. The main thing is that he/she should be able to use this generosity wisely.

Deer Man

The charming man of the Deer sign is always at the center of attention. Attracts women with his courtesy and fine manners. At the same time, he feels the core, the ability to protect, surround with care and love. Rivals respect the man of this sign for the firmness of character and honesty. Surrounding people agree in one opinion: a worthy, decent person. Easily goes through life and happily avoids failures. But if he suddenly finds himself in a difficult situation, he loses control of his feelings and shows anger and aggression.

Deer Woman

The woman of the sign Deer seems too many to be too narcissistic and proud. Only close people can she reveal the secrets of her soul and share experiences and doubts. A shy, suspicious nature often doubts her strength and painfully accepts failures. Feels safe only in comfortable conditions and strives for a luxurious life. Often she devotes too much time to the material component, forgetting about the soul. Nature endowed her with many talents: a woman of the sign Deer can cope with all problems if she trusts her intuition and believes in her strength.

World-famous people born on Deer Day

Kurt Vonnegut (b. 11/11/1922) – A cult American writer.

Alessandro Cagliostro (b. 06/2/1743) – A well-known mystic and charlatan sorcerer.

Johnny Depp (b. 06/09/1963) – Cult Hollywood actor.

Elton John (b. 03/25/1947) – British popular singer.

Nikita Bogoslovsky (b. 05/22/1913) – Popular Russian composer

Ludwig van Beethoven (b. 12/17/1770) – Brilliant German composer

Robert Scott (b. 6.06.1868) – English polar explorer.

Immanuel Kant (b. 04/22/1724) – German philosopher and founder of classical philosophy.

Chapter 12 – Sunrise (Lamat).

Name: Q´ANIL / Lamat (Lamat)
Meaning: Star, Moon, Rabbit
Element: Fire
Direction: South
Compatibility: Sunrise, Ladder, Vulture, Lord, Grain

The meaning of the Mayan symbol

Those born on March 3, March 28, April 17, May 7, May 27, June 16, July 6, July 26, August 15, September 4, September 24, October 14, November 3, November 23, December 13, 2 January, January 22, February 11 in the Mayan Zodiac is called LAMAT (Sunrise).

Sometimes you can find another name for this sign – Rabbit, but this name is Aztec and has nothing to do with the Mayan calendar.

Mayan LAMAT means "radiance" or "Star of the Sunrise." The word also refers to the planet Venus, which ends the night and precedes the sunrise. Another meaning of the Mayan root "lam" is "ending, completion."

The main element of the hieroglyph of the Mayan sign of Sunrise is four circles in the four corners of the sign, diverging from the center. In the language of graphic symbols, this expresses the idea of abundance, completeness, and completeness.

In a broad sense, the sign of the Sunrise should be understood as a symbol of completion, bringing to the end everything that was hatched earlier – whether it is the final maturation of the fetus in the womb or the completion of previously started cases.

Sunrise character

The character of our modern civilization, with all its advantages and disadvantages, is best embodied in the person of the Sunrise. Wherever he or she is in whatever situation he or she finds oneself, he/she will always remain a modern person in the full sense of the word.

A person of the Sunrise does not tend to sit idly by – Nature itself has determined in such a way that a thirst for activity always ripens in his/her soul. This thirst is so great that when he or she cannot realize it for one reason or another, he/she runs the risk of falling into pessimism or depression. However, much more often, a person of the Sunrise still finds a use for his/her active nature.

Perhaps the main feature of his/her character is practicality and concreteness. The Sunrise person is not inclined to abstract philosophies. He or she does not like obscurity and unfinished business. His/her formula is "time is money", according to which one tries to build one's life.

All this leads to the fact that the person of Sunrise is always looking for the simplest and shortest ways to implement his/her ideas. He or she does not like to complicate the situation because, first, efficiency is important, for which he/she is ready to sacrifice a lot.

The Sunrise person is determined to get the maximum result at the minimum cost, even at the expense of quality. He/she does not seek to leave his/her mark on the ages. But here's what's interesting: although the things one takes on are not always as perfect as Swiss watches, due to their simplicity and efficiency, they often look no less attractive than the outstanding works of great masters.

Under these qualities, a person of the Sunrise knows how to earn money. He/she was born to become a good professional in his/her field because professionalism is not about doing the impossible but making the best use of the available resources. At the same time, one needs to achieve results quickly with minimal effort and money. He or she will not throw all his/her resources to achieve the goal – if his/her goal requires too much effort, the person of Sunrise will simply choose another one for himself/herself, and he or she will gladly spend the free time on himself/herself.

In general, about money, the person of the Sunrise is by no means a hoarder. Of course, he or she is not averse to earning more, but he/she can quite be satisfied with what one has. Often people of this sign generally spend more than they earn, not being afraid to live on credit and not particularly thinking about the future in this regard. Their life credo comes down to a simple thought: we live once, meaning we must have time to try everything.

In addition, such features as independence and the desire to live with his mind characterize the person of the Sunrise. He/she loves and values his/her freedom, for which he or she is ready to fight. At the same time, having become addicted, he/she will not limit oneself to dreams of freedom, but will begin to actively look for a specific way out – and, due to his/her practicality; most likely, he or she will find this way out.

In business, this usually manifests itself in the fact that even if a Sunrise person has to work for someone, he/she will try to simultaneously carry out one`s affairs, as managers of all large companies usually do. If such an opportunity presents itself, he/she will most likely prefer to start his/her own business, where only one will be the boss to him/her.

In general, a person of Sunrise always puts his/her goals and interests at the forefront, and in any circumstances, he or she is ready to defend them, acting decisively and toughly. Undoubtedly, the expression: "Nothing personal, it's just business" was invented by the people of Sunrise.

The independence and love of freedom of a person of this sign are expressed in the desire to live with his/her mind and freethinking. There are no taboo topics for him/her. He or she does not like to hide one's thoughts behind florid vague phrases, preferring to speak directly about his/her thoughts, and can openly discuss any sensitive topics, whether politics or sex.

In turn, the tendency to frankness and directness inherent in the person of Sunrise often provokes conflicts around him/her. In the eyes of others, he or she sometimes looks too harsh because his/her sign does not imply such features as restraint and delicacy. The Sunrise person is not accustomed to keeping oneself within the framework of any conventions.

However, there are many advantages to this direct communication style. In a relationship with such a person, there is no room for ambiguity: he or she is predictable, and you know what to expect from him/her. Perhaps the person of the Sunrise is used to dividing the world into black and white, but it can be said with all certainty that oriental cunning is not his/her style.

At the same time, Sunrise's desire to simplify the situation has its downside because often, the easiest way to get away from the problem comes down to relieving tension with the help of alcohol or drugs. At the same time, his or her independence from Sunrise does little to persuade him/her to listen to the experience of others and opinions on this matter. That is why they should be very careful that dubious "simple pleasures" do not ruin their life.

Similar simplicity, looseness, and freethinking are fully inherent in the person of the Sunrise in sexual relations. The sign's energy does not incline him/her to restraint in this matter; conservative family values are usually alien to him/her. Usually, a person of Sunrise stands for an open relationship in love, not bothering his/her collaborate with excessive jealousy and expecting the same from him/her. Marriage, for him/her, is primarily a form of partnership, and only then everything else. That is why, most often, people of Sunrise prefer such a frank and ambiguous form of relationship between spouses as a marriage contract.

In general, this sign is quite favorable for a career and life in our modern, full of contradictions world. After all, a person of Sunrise, like no one else, has absorbed all its advantages and disadvantages and feels oneself in it no worse than a fish in water.

Man Sunrise

The man of the Sunrise sign carefully monitors his appearance: he is always neatly combed and smart dressed. He is an object of adoration for women, an object of desire. He has a sharp mind and an excellent memory. Despite his straightforwardness, he will find a way to get around an awkward situation. Therefore, it is considered a good speaker with whom it is pleasant to spend time. But in a critical situation, his brazen complacency is instantly replaced by composure and concentration. First, he is a businessperson; everything else is completely unimportant.

Woman Sunrise

A touching, sensitive woman of the Star sign needs a strong partner. She can build a successful career if desired but strives to create a strong family. In dreams, she sees herself as a mother of a bunch of children, a real keeper of a home hearth. She has a culinary talent and cooks a lot and deliciously. She uses natural abilities with maximum benefit: the house is a full bowl, and the garden strikes the imagination with fragrant flowers and outlandish plants. A modest woman rejoices in the happiness of close people and fully dedicates herself to their interests. But do not forget about her practical approach to life: at the very beginning of family relations, it is she who will be the first to start talking about a marriage contract.

World Celebrities Born on Sunrise Day

Elvis Presley (b. 01/08/1935) – The king of rock and roll.

Jimi Hendrix (b. 11/27/1942) – American guitarist, singer, composer, and electric guitar pioneer.

Whitney Houston (b. 08/09/1963) – American singer, film actress.

Julio Iglesias (b. 09/23/1943) – The most popular Spanish singer of the 80-90s.

Sergey Obraztsov (b. 07/05/1901) – The famous Russian theater director-puppeteer.

Mother Teresa (b. 08/27/1910) – A public figure who has become a symbol of mercy.

Roald Amundsen (b. 07/16/1872) – Norwegian polar explorer, the first to reach the South Pole.

Sydney Sheldon (b. 02/11/1917) – American writer.

Yaroslav Gashek (b. 04/30/1883) – Czech satirist, author of The Adventures of Schweik.

Alexandre Dumas father (b. 07/24/1802) – French writer, author of the novels, *The Three Musketeers, The Count of Monte Cristo*, etc.

Honore de Balzac (p. 05/20/1799) – French writer distinguished by extraordinary fertility.

Chapter 13 – Water (Muluk).

Name: TOOJ / Muluk
Meaning: Water, Rain, Fish
Element: Earth
Direction: East
Compatibility: World Tree, Reed, Earthquake, Serpent

The meaning of the Mayan symbol

Those born on March 4, March 29, April 18, May 8, May 28, June 17, July 7, July 27, August 16, September 5, September 25, October 15, November 4, November 24, December 14, 3 January, January 23, February 12 in the Mayan Zodiac is called MULUK (water).

The Mayan MULUK means "reserve of water" or simply "reserve from the root "mul" – "to collect" and "uk" – "drink." The Aztec counterpart of this sign is Atl, "water." Because both the Yucatec Maya and the Aztecs lived in arid territories, water was one of their main values, without which life would be simply impossible.

The main element of the hieroglyph Muluk is a drop depicted as a small circle in the center. This sign was used in Mayan texts not only to depict water but also in general reserves as such, sometimes on the hieroglyph Muluk, for example, in the Cartesian Code, there is a symbolic image of an open palm, which holds the same drop in the form of a circle. This whole image expresses the idea of collecting and receiving something.

In a broad sense, this sign expresses the idea of hidden resources that the body accumulates in case of any critical situations.

Water Character

Water is one of the most controversial and therefore misinterpreted signs. Indeed, a person born on this day has such an unusual character that his /her behavior often seems strange and illogical to those around him/her. But this is only at first glance. The bottom line is that Nature itself endowed the Waterman with very large internal resources, but these resources are extremely difficult for him/her to use in everyday life – they turn on only at critical moments.

All this leads to the fact that a person of Water often looks slow, sluggish even lazy, in ordinary life. However, in difficult periods of life, a person of Water, unexpectedly for everyone – including himself/herself – awakens a surprisingly powerful energy that helps him/her find a way out. This is where the advantage of the person of Water over everyone else usually manifests oneself.

In life, this is manifested in the fact that a person of Water is often surprised to notice how hard it is for him / her to do the most seemingly elementary things that others do easily and simply. Take at least such an ordinary thing as the habit of going to work every day and constantly being busy with something useful. For most people, this is as natural as breathing. But not for the person of Water. For him/her, these simple rules require too much tension, from which he or she quickly gets tired and, therefore, often neglects generally accepted norms.

It is not surprising that with such an attitude to the matter, everyday difficulties and troubles can fall on a person of Water like from a leaky bag. But this is precisely the paradox of his/her character, that these same difficulties mobilize him/her, forcing him/her to show miracles of quickness and energy. Simply put, this person has a unique ability to successfully overcome the problems one creates for oneself. It is interesting that a person of Water, knowing this feature behind him/her, can create difficulties for himself consciously! Therefore, the artist Salvador Dali, born on this day, could not work in calm conditions. To create his/her paintings, one deliberately exhausted one with lack of sleep – only in this semi-conscious state was his/her world-famous masterpieces born.

At the same time, although the person of Water oneself, in ordinary conditions, is prone to slowness and neglect of the rules; he/she often expects quite the opposite from others. He or she can sometimes be very demanding of those around him/her, not noticing the beam in his/her eye.

However, the exactingness of his/her, like all his/her behavior, is not particularly consistent. In a complacent mood, a person of Water can turn a blind eye to the shortcomings and mistakes of others for a long time and then suddenly impute them to blame, demanding immediate correction. Naturally, this style of communication is not always effective.

The Water person is very partial to wealth in all its forms. But if wealth is a means for obtaining life's blessings for others, then the idea of accumulation is important for a person of Water. In this matter, he/she can be completely insatiable. At the same time, it is interesting that the Water person cares little about effectively using what has been accumulated. Often it gives him pleasure to possess the most seemingly useless things, justifying this desire with a simple motto: "Maybe come in handy."

Such promiscuity in accumulation can manifest itself in anything – from collecting unnecessary things to the aimless accumulation of knowledge in various fields. But what is surprising is that many of these things or knowledge can come in handy at the most unexpected moment because he or she, like no one else, has the talent to turn trash into something useful if necessary, finding unusual uses for things. In a word, if there is a magician in the world who can turn garbage into gold, he/she was surely born under the sign of Water.

Regarding money, a person of Water often also behaves inconsistently. In business, one can be tight-fisted, even stingy, but sometimes he/she can surprise others with his suddenly awakened generosity. However, in general, one is dominated by the desire to create reserves for the future. And often, he/she succeeds. So, it was during the reign of the representative of the Water Sign, Bill Clinton, that America's wealth reached his highest level in its entire history.

Of course, in the eyes of others (and often in their own), the person of Water looks very contradictory. His / her behavior can be annoying with its inconsistency and illogicality. Nevertheless, it is wrong to be seriously offended by him /her because such a character is inherent by Nature itself, which has special plans for him /her. It's just that it was not created to live life with maximum convenience but to use its colossal internal resources in difficult times to solve super-tasks, coming to the rescue of others.

Man Water

It is difficult for people around to recognize a man's character with the sign of Water; this is such a contradictory nature. A hesitant, soft person seems too easy prey for a domineering woman. But if necessary, it can show firmness and exactingness. It cannot be called a trouble-free, ready-for-everything partner. In the depths of his soul, a man of the sign of Water builds ambitious plans. He simply does not consider it necessary to share them with everyone. Strives for a comfortable life, passionately desires popularity and fame, and possesses all the necessary qualities.

Woman Water

A woman of the sign of Water tends to exaggerate problems, often doubts her strength, and is completely in vain. She has powerful internal potential and can overcome any obstacles. Needs a strong partner to whom she will devote himself without a trace. But there will likely be many chosen ones: too susceptible to passions, completely surrendered to feelings. She has fragile health, so she devotes a lot of time to his physical condition, forgetting about the soul. But the hidden possibilities can give her strength in life's most difficult moments.

World Celebrities Born on Water Day

John Lennon (b. 9/10/1940)- Founder and member of the cult rock band "The Beatles". One of the most popular musicians of the 20th century.

John Travolta (b. 02/18/1954)- Popular Hollywood actor.

Jennifer Lopez (b. 07/24/1970)– Popular American singer, actress, and businesswoman.

Madonna (b. 08/16/1958)- The infamous American pop star.

Mick Jagger (b. 07/26/1943)- English rock musician and founder of the Rolling Stones.

Oprah Winfrey (b. 01/29/1954)- One of America's most popular TV presenters.

Wolfgang Amadeus Mozart (b. 01/27/1756)– Great Austrian composer, a classic of world music.

William Shakespeare (b. 04/23/1564)- A brilliant English poet and playwright, a classic of world drama.

Salvador Dali (b. 05/11/1904)– Famous Spanish surrealist artist.

George Washington (b. 02/22/1732)- First President of the United States, Commander-in-Chief of the American Army during the Revolutionary War

Bill Clinton (b. 08/19/1946)- 41st President of the United States.

Saddam Hussein (b. 04/28/1937)- Iraqi dictator.

Al Capone (b. 01/17/1899) was One of the most famous American gangsters.

Ernesto Che Guevara (b. 06/14/1928)- A Latin American revolutionary who has become a global symbol of a fighter for justice.

Chapter 14 – Dog (Ok).

Name: T´ZI / Oc (Ook)
Meaning: Dog, Leg
Element: Air
Direction: North
Compatibility: Dog, Jaguar, Flint, Wind, Scull

The meaning of the Mayan symbol

Those born on March 5, March 30, April 19, May 9, May 29, June 18, July 8, July 28, August 17, September 6, September 26, October 16, November 5, November 25, December 15, 4 January, January 24, February 13 in the Mayan Zodiac is called **Ok (Dog).**

Mayan OK means, "step," "path," and "move," but it can also be understood in the meaning of "traveler" and "tramp." For example, the Mayan expression "ah oks" means "going". In Maya-K'iche, this sign is called "Qi" and has several meanings: "dog," as well as "willful," and "imprudent." The hieroglyph of the Mayan sign is OK depicts a dog's head, in which a stylized dog paw print is inscribed. This figure should be understood as an indication of restlessness, a penchant for adventure and travel.

Often, the hieroglyph of the Ok sign around the dog's mouth shows a chain of black dots, which expresses the idea of verbosity and increased emotionality. The Book of Signs of the Days also speaks of this, pointing out that one of the signs of this day is forty.

Thus, the sign symbolizes such qualities and traits as curiosity and curiosity combined with increased emotionality.

Dog Character

The main feature of a person born on the day of the Dog is his /her emotions' special brightness and strength. He/she has such a strong emotionality that it determines his /her entire character, behavior, and lifestyle. This does not mean that such a concept as logic is alien to him /her. On the contrary, the Dog has a very mobile mind, learns quickly, and has a good memory. It's just that his/her thinking is emotional. Dry dispassionate reasoning alienates him /her, and he/she often trusts his/her inner instinct more than logical calculations.

A good example of this is one of the greatest chess players in the world, Robert Fischer, who was born under the sign of the Dog. Nobody managed to beat him. Nevertheless, despite his intellectual abilities, Fisher was distinguished by extreme emotionality, now and then becoming the center of all sorts of scandals.

Due to this heightened emotionality inherent, the Dog person often has childish features for life. Often, until old age, he/she does not lose his/her sincere ability to be surprised and enjoy life. At heart, he/she is a romantic who finds it difficult to sit still and whose life is always calling for new adventures. Such craving can manifest itself in all areas of his/her life.

Like any temperamental person, the routine of everyday life not only disgusts the Dog but also can even negatively affect his/her health. After all, the main engine of his vitality is emotions and feelings that need constant renewal. Without it, they just fade away. In turn, extinguished emotions for a Dog-person mean a lack of vitality. In this state, he or she, like no one else, risks falling into a deep depression. However, most people of this sign know or feel this feature behind them and therefore find themselves on certain adventures that bring the necessary variety to their lives.

The Dog person's propensity for adventure is often fully manifested in his/her love. Due to his/her sincerity, he or she is not disposed to betrayal, but it can be difficult for him/her to tame his or her sensual nature. Nevertheless, it does not mean that the Dog person has no choice but to look for diversity on the side. Often, these people prefer to openly negotiate with a partner about freedom in their relationship to avoid stepping to him or her, but this is not the only possible option. It's just that here you need to remember a simple rule: to bind a Dog person to oneself, in no case should you allow a love relationship with him/her to turn into a routine – otherwise, his/her cooling can happen quickly and abruptly. Try to turn love with him/her into an interesting game. Don't be afraid to tease and provoke. In a word, play with him or her like a big child, stirring his senses. Be sure that, in this case, the sincerity and loyalty inherent in the Dog will manifest itself with all possible force.

Similarly, the Dog person feels himself/herself in the professional field. He/she is a romantic and a dreamer, and believes me; the last thing he/she dreams of is spending his/her life in a dusty office, shifting papers from place to place. Do not believe it, even if he/she tells you that such work is his or her dream. This is just bravado. The emotionality and restlessness of people of this sign are manifested in the fact that, most often, they are attracted to work related to creativity or adventure. So, one of the brightest representatives of the Dog sign, in his/her youth, chose intelligence as his/her profession – that is, an area shrouded in a halo of romance. Today his name – Vladimir Putin – is known all over the world.

Another feature of the Dog sign is the gift of eloquence. It is very unlikely that communication with a person born on this day will inspire boredom. On the contrary, due to his /her temperament, he/she can bring a live stream into any conversation on any topic.

Perhaps, among the shortcomings of the Dog, only two can be distinguished. Firstly, this is intemperance, which in a Dog person can manifest in anything – in an attraction to delicious food, carnal pleasures, or alcohol. Often these people, in their enthusiasm, can lose all sense of proportion. Secondly, the increased emotionality of the Dog often provokes conflict situations. These people rarely watch their words and may use too harsh, offensive expressions for the speaker. In a word, it is difficult to suspect them of an excess of diplomacy.

Naturally, all this complicates the life of a person of this sign, so if he/she wants his /her fate and career to develop more favorably, he/she does not interfere with learning to control, if not his /her feelings, then at least one`s behavior and words. In this case, his or her numerous talents, the ability to learn quickly and grasp the very essence of the issue on the fly will surely provide him/her with a worthy place in life, and one`s lively, vivid emotions and sincere nature will always attract a large number of friends and allies to him /her.

Male Dog

A decent man of the Dog sign causes respect, and the people around him treat him with sympathy. He tries to maintain good relations with everyone, but sometimes he is unrestrained in the manifestation of his feelings. It can easily offend a person with a careless word, but not out of a desire to offend – it simply expresses its opinion. His irrepressible vitality and desire to experience only joyful emotions are the causes of misfortunes and misfortunes.

Easily falls into dependence on bad habits and can become an alcoholic.

Woman Dog

A bright, showy woman, A Dog, is an object of admiration and worship. She likes to dress up. The best gift for her is an exquisite piece of jewelry. Has a strong intuition and easily guesses the mood of people. Natural sexuality makes her a little illegible in relationships. Strives to get the whole range of emotions from life, but in marriage, she manifests herself as a faithful, devoted wife. Always defends the interests of close people and takes care of their well-being. Despite some frivolity, she soberly assesses her capabilities and correctly sets life priorities.

Celebrities Born on Dog Day

Mark Twain (b. 11/30/1835) – American classic writer, master of humorous pamphlets.

Steven Spielberg (b. 12/18/1946) – Cult American director.

Gerard Depardieu (b. 12/27/1948) – French actor.

Sharon Stone (b. 03/10/1958) – One of the sexiest and most intelligent actresses in Hollywood history.

Pamela Anderson (b. 07/01/1967) – American actress, sex symbol of the 90s.

Eddie Murphy (b. 04/03/1961) – A popular Hollywood actor of the comic genre.

David Copperfield (b. 09/16/1956) – American illusionist and magician.

Bob Marley (b. 02/06/1945) – American musician, a native of Jamaica.

Bobby Fischer (b. 03/09/1943) – The great American chess player, the genius of the chessboard.

Robert Oppenheimer (b. 04/22/1904) – American physicist who led the work on the creation of the atomic bomb.

Max Planck (b. 04/23/1858) – German physicist, one of the founders of quantum theory.

Chapter 15 – Master (Chuen).

Name: B´AATZ / Chuen
Meaning: Monkey, Master
Element: Water
Direction: West
Compatibility: Master, Opel, Storm, Night, Deer

The meaning of the Mayan symbol

Those born on March 6, March 31, April 20, May 10, May 30, June 19, July 9, July 29, August 18, September 7, September 27, October 17, November 6, November 26, December 16, 5 January, January 25, February 14 in the Mayan Zodiac is called Chuen (Master).

The Maya-K'iche and the Aztecs call this sign Monkey, but the Mayan Chuen means "skillful," which comes from the root that means "to fill." The hieroglyph of the sign Chuen symbolically depicts an open mouth with teeth.

Often inside the mouth, there is a sign of grain (in the form of a rectangle divided into two parts) and an image of a vessel for storing supplies.

In some texts, the hieroglyph of this sign contains only a mouth with three teeth. Among the Mayan Indians, the number three (Mayan "osh") has always been used the meaning "many," and "toothy" (Mayan "ah ko" or "ko ol") also has the meaning "strong," "capable," so it is obvious that the image of a mouth with three teeth expresses the idea of an abundance of strength and ability.

Thus, the sign of the Master, Chuen, expresses the idea of an abundance of strength, abilities, and talents.

The character of the Master

Nature has generously endowed a person born under the sign of the Master with talents and abilities in various fields. He/she easily and naturally gives those things to which others have to go with patient labor. He/she knows how to think quickly, grasps the essence of the issue on the fly, is very insightful, and his or her conclusions, as a rule, are amazingly accurate. However, there is a catch in the same lightness: such lightness relaxes. A person born under this sign often has no incentive to realize their many talents. It turns out a paradox: having from Nature much greater abilities than others do, the Master has less desire to realize them.

A person with this sign often has such a trait as self-satisfaction. In the depths of his soul, the Master knows very well or at least guesses about his/her extraordinary abilities and even about his or her superiority over others. He/she sees that much in life is given to him /her without much difficulty, and often this alone is quite enough for him or her. And this is annoying because any talent without application can stall. Just as muscles gradually lose strength without regular training, so over time, the Master can lose his /her talents or squander them on trifles.

As for the attitude to his/her numerous talents, the Master can express it in different ways. He/she considers his /her high abilities to be something natural and therefore underestimates them. In this case, he or she can sincerely believe that others have talents no less than him /her and that Fate has prepared the path of the most ordinary person who has no chance of achieving special success. Such disbelief in oneself will not allow him /her to achieve significant results, but only Nature will be to blame for this.

However, it also happens that in the depths of his /her soul, the Master feels his superiority over others. It often annoys him /her that it is difficult for people to understand some things that seem obvious and simple. Over time, it can develop into such unpleasant traits as arrogance and even arrogance.

The fate of the Master is most favorable if life itself forces one not to sit back but to strain and move forward – in this case, he/she can achieve tremendous success.

So, for the famous Hollywood actress Barbara Streisand, born on the day of the Master, such an incentive, in her own words, was an ugly appearance. All her life, she strove to assert herself – both in her own eyes and in the eyes of others. And here's what's interesting: not having a Hollywood smile or sex appeal and having, it would seem, no chance of becoming a superstar, she nevertheless became one.

However, not only life's difficulties can become a driving force for the Master. It is enough that some strong interest or powerful hobby appears in one's life, which will lead him/her out of a state of happy contentment and doing nothing. This is exactly what happened to the famous French oenologist Jacques-Yves Cousteau, born on the day of the Master, who from childhood was so fascinated by the beauties and secrets of the underwater world that he devoted his whole life to them. And on this path, the Master's talents were useful to him as well as possible. Indeed, to achieve his cherished dream, he invented scuba gear on the go, doing it almost with the same ease with which we collect a travel bag when we hit the road.

In a word, the talents possessed by people born today are impressive. The main thing is to use them, not let them fade away.

In other words, if the Master wants to succeed in life, he/she should remember that talent is not everything. This is just an advance Nature gives him /her, which one will have to justify by finding a worthy application. And if he or she manages to overcome his /her weakness, then the generous Fate, no doubt, will open before him /her all possible doors leading to success.

Male Master

A charming, physically attractive man of the Master sign is of great interest to women who dream of getting married. A cheerful, emotional person can give a good mood. Talent, luck, and hard work are the components of his success. A financially secure person does not spare money for gifts. He often arranges surprises for his loved ones. He does not make strict requirements for close people. He just waits for admiration.

Woman Master

The woman of the Master sign is a coquette. Some consider her a frivolous person. Creative nature is in captivity of dreams and fantasies and does not differ in housekeeping and practicality. In difficult life situations, her natural luck invariably helps. Happily lives a life surrounded by close people. She rarely rushes from one extreme to another: he quickly lights up with an idea and instantly cools down. Just a couple of days ago, she talked about a theater career. Today she dreams of going on a sea cruise to write from nature. Strives to find a strong, reliable partner who can wisely guide her through life.

World celebrities born on the day of the Master

Johann Sebastian Bach (b. 03/21/1685) – Great German classical composer.

Hans Christian Andersen (b. 2.04.1805) – Danish storyteller, author of the books "Thumbelina", "The Snow Queen", etc.

Michael Faraday (b. 09/22/1791) – English physicist and chemist, brilliant self-taught scientist.

Ronald Reagan (b. 02/06/1911) – 40th President of the United States.

Stanley Kubrick (b. 07/26/1928) – One of the greatest American directors of the late twentieth century.

Harrison Ford (b. 07/13/1942) – Cult Hollywood actor.

Robert DeNiro (b. 08/17/1943) – American film actor, one of the most talented actors of his generation.

Barbara Streisand (b. 04/24/1942) – Hollywood theater and film actress.

Dustin Hoffman (b. 08/08/1937) – American actor and producer.

David Bowie (b. 01/08/1947) – Cult British rock musician, singer, actor, and composer.

World war.

Neil Armstrong (b. 08/05/1930) – American astronaut, the first man to land on the moon.

Jacques-Yves Cousteau (b. 06/11/1910) – French oceanographer, inventor of scuba gear.

Chapter 16 – Ladder (EB).

Name: EE / Eb (Eb)
Meaning: Road, Grass, Scull
Element: Fire
Direction: South
Compatibility: Ladder, Vulture, Overlord, Grain, Sunrise

The meaning of the Mayan symbol

Those born on March 7, April 1, April 21, May 11, May 31, June 20, July 10, July 30, August 19, September 8, September 28, October 18, November 7, November 27, December 17, 6 January, January 26, February 15 in the Mayan Zodiac is called EB (Ladder).

Mayan EB means "ladder." The Maya Quiche call this same sign Evob – "teeth," and the Aztecs have two names for it at once: Itlan – "teeth," and Mullinali – "a bunch of grass, a broom." Even though among the Yucatec Maya, the main meaning of this word is still "ladder;" nevertheless, its hieroglyph also depicts a tooth surrounded by black dots, which is a conventional designation of a row of teeth (on Mayan pictograms, a series of dots surrounding an object denotes a plural number).

At first glance, all these symbols – a ladder, teeth, a bunch of grass – seem to be separate, but they are united by one common idea: they all symbolically express such concepts as compatibility, unity, and orderliness.

In general, the sign of the Ladder expresses the idea of order, organization, and community.

Character of the Ladder

The main feature inherent in a person born under the sign of the Ladder is his/her internal organization. This person belongs to that rare breed of people who never forget to take their fishing rods when they go fishing. Such organization is manifested in all possible areas: he/she is logical, does not like unnecessary fuss, and his /her views, as a rule, are distinguished by constancy. Perhaps ideal order does not reign in his things, but the person of the Ladder always knows exactly where and what he/her has.

All these qualities in our chaotic world can hardly be called useless. Moreover, the organization of the person of Ladder often helps him/her succeed in various fields. He/she is a born organizer and leader who cannot only give commands to others but is also ready to obey the established rules oneself.

The clarity of thought and logic inherent in the Ladder person can help him/her make a career in many areas. At the same time, one cannot be called a boring cracker – on the contrary, one is quite emotional and may well find himself/herself even in creative professions. The paradox lies in the fact that his/her deep emotions do not at all prevent him/her from thinking clearly and analyzing the situation.

The Ladder person is fully characterized by such traits as compassion and the ability to sympathize. Sometimes he/she can worry too deeply about one's own and other people's troubles, taking them to heart. Even when he/she looks stern and adamant outwardly, be sure that behind this mask lies a very compassionate soul; just difficulties and hard experiences have made his/her character tough.

A Ladder is a good family person. Usually, people of this sign put the family's interests above their own because selfishness is alien to their nature. It happens that they show excessive severity to family members, but genuine love and care are always hidden behind this severity.

Another feature of the Ladder is that a person born on this day, like no one else, believes in justice. One's nature determined that his/her thoughts about how exactly our world should be arranged predominately.

Thinking about good and evil, about what is good and what is bad, how people (including himself) should behave – all this is very characteristic of the Ladder person. It is no coincidence that the greatest classic of world literature, Leo Tolstoy, was born under this sign, and it is no coincidence that the theme of morality occupies a central place in all his works. And the fact that even before the abolition of serfdom, Tolstoy gave freedom to his peasants, left with practically nothing, also speaks volumes.

In general, the Ladder is the most "socialist," in the good sense of this word. Nevertheless, the desire of the Ladder for justice is not always easy to realize, and the point is not that people do not want to live by fair laws but that everyone understands justice in their way. The area of morality affects emotions, and it is often pointless to look for logic where there are emotions. That is why the desire of the Ladder to restore order where passions rage and where everyone has their idea of good and evil is, in most cases, doomed to failure. This can greatly complicate his or her life and exhaust his/her nerves.

This is where the main danger of this sign lies because it is not in vain that they say. The road to hell is paved with good intentions. The excessive desire of the person of the Ladder to change the world for the better, and the difficulties that await him or her on this path, can irritate both him/her and those around him or her. On this slippery slope, it is not long to slide down to meaningless moralism. In order not to spoil the life of oneself or others, one can simply advise the person of the Ladder to use the main gospel commandment: do not judge, but accept people as they are. Love changes the world for the better, much more than any morality.

In other words, the person on the Ladder does not interfere with somehow softening or balancing his/her increased demands on him or her and others. Having learned to be indulgent to small human weaknesses, he/she has every chance to achieve the necessary harmony with the world around him/her and live a long, happy life.

In general, the sign of the Ladder has a very powerful influence on people. It is not surprising that a person born on this day will be fascinated by the problems of politics or religion, but in any case, his or her organization, logic, clarity of thinking, and love of order can help him/her reach the proper heights. His/her life may turn out differently, but one thing is certain: he/she will not waste it on trifles.

Man Ladder

A confident, unflappable man of the sign is a reliable support for a fragile, vulnerable woman. He only has to fall in love, as ardent passion instantly replaces restraint. He may be too carried away by the search for his only one, so there are many novels behind him. A purposeful man builds ambitious plans and tries to be in the profession. The results of his work are material wealth and household comfort. He generously shares them with loved ones.

Woman Ladder

The woman of the sign boldly steps along the winding path of life. He tries to behave noble and dignifiedly but sometimes makes frivolous acquaintances. Numerous amorous hobbies do not affect the quality of work. A smart, serious woman is a careerist focused on her work. Nevertheless, close people do not feel deprived of warmth and care. After a hard-working day, she will be interested in their mood and well-being. Representatives of this sign love to have long conversations, sometimes, they are too fond of collecting gossip, but not for idle pleasure: they are trying to find out the truth.

World famous people born on Ladder Day.

Karl Marx (b. 05/05/1818) – German philosopher, economist, and the main ideologist of communism.

George Gordon Byron (b. 01/22/1788) – English romantic poet.

Robert Stevenson (b. 11/13/1850) – English writer, author of adventure books "Treasure Island", etc.

O. Henry (b. 09/11/1862) – American classic writer.

Dwight Eisenhower (b. 10/14/1890) – 34th President of the United States.

Chapter 17 – Reed (B`en).

Name: AAJ / B`en (Ben)
Meaning: Maize, Reed, Cane
Element: Earth
Direction: East
Compatibility: World Tree, Earthquake, Serpent, Water

The meaning of the Mayan symbol

Those born on March 8, April 2, April 22, May 12, June 1, June 21, July 11, July 31, August 20, September 9, September 29, October 19, November 8, November 28, December 18, 7 January, January 27, February 16 in the Mayan Zodiac is called B`EN (Reed).

The Mayan word B`EN comes from a root meaning, "to go" The B`en sign expresses the idea of purposeful growth. Therefore, in the "Book of Signs of the Days" one of this day's signs is "sprouting."

The Maya Quiche and the Aztecs call this sign Reed, which in figurative language has the same meaning since the main feature of the breed is its intense, purposeful growth. Unlike a tree, which develops upwards and breadth, a reed grows exclusively in one direction.

The hieroglyph of the sign B`en symbolically depicts reeds growing in several rows, one row higher than the other. The lower row of reeds rests on a double horizontal line, while the upper row grows above it. This image expresses the idea of super-intensive growth, overgrowing, and going beyond all limits and boundaries.

In other words, the B`en sign is a sign of purposeful striving for something, a sign of non-stop, steady growth.

Reed character

A person born under the sign of the Reed is not used to stopping there. Concepts like "enough" or "a little bit of good" are not for him/her, and often the word "better" means "more." Nature has determined in such a way that the main thing for him/her is the very idea of growth and increase in everything, no matter what he/she undertakes.

One main feature distinguishing Reed is his/her extreme perseverance in achieving the goal. There are no barriers; one is ready to move forward, even if, for this, he/she has to confront the whole world. On this road, thorns do not frighten him or her. Just as grass, in its unbridled growth, can break through powerful asphalt and concrete, so the person of the Reed is used to getting his/her way, regardless of difficulties.

Such qualities can only be envied. Thanks to his/her patience and penetrating abilities, Reed can make an excellent career in almost any field, but for this, like no one else, he/she needs to choose the right path independently from the very beginning. The fact is that once having chosen some direction, this person is not inclined to retreat, and therefore, if the direction was chosen incorrectly, he/she risks spending life on fruitless attempts, as they say, to break through an impenetrable wall with his/her forehead. After all, just as zealously as he/she strives for his goal, one can persist in his/her own mistakes.

With all this, it cannot be said that Reed is not at all characterized by such a quality as flexibility. On the contrary, he/she can be very resourceful, finding unexpected ways and loopholes where others do not even notice them. Often these people are distinguished by a very flexible, even quirky mind. The consistency and constancy of Reed are manifested in the fact that all this happens within the framework of one general direction, which he/she has chosen and from which he or she does not intend to deviate.

Due to his/her character as lack of a sense of proportion and perseverance, it can be difficult for a Reed person to stop in time. In addition, he/she has a rare talent, as they say, "to make an elephant out of a fly." A minor misunderstanding that another would not pay attention to can develop into a serious offense. Those around may not even guess what feelings are ripening in his/her soul until they reach considerable strength and splash out one day. Then it will be extremely difficult to correct the misunderstanding.

That is why in relation to Reed, it is advisable to avoid unsaid moments, remembering that his/her thoughts and feelings are remarkably constancy. He/she never forgets anything and can remember even a minor offense all his/her life.

However, the same constancy of feelings is characteristic in good things. Like no one else, one knows the value of friendly feelings and how to be a devoted friend.

Due to their characteristics, people of this sign make good professionals. Perhaps their knowledge and views are not particularly broad, but they know almost everything in their field. Moreover, they constantly increase their professional knowledge and skills, becoming truly excellent specialists.

Like no one else, Reed knows how to focus on his/her work, not be distracted by trifles, and never abandon the work he/she has begun halfway. All these qualities, combined with patience, diligence, and the ability to work well and a lot, certainly help him/her succeed. Often these people, in the full sense of the word, make themselves rising to the heights from the very bottom.

Another feature of Reed is his/her observation and concreteness. One knows how to notice things that elude the attention of others and can put them to good use, turning a trifle into something meaningful and useful. At the same time, a huge plus is that Reed is not prone to ambiguity and vague wording but can clearly express his or her thoughts. Even in those areas where it would seem difficult to concretize anything and everything seems unsteady and vague, Reed can find the necessary "solid support" and specifics.

A striking example of such an amazing ability is the fact that both the great founders of psychoanalysis – Sigmund Freud and Carl Gustav Jung – were born on the day of the Reed. And indeed, these people managed to bring a clear logic to where misunderstanding and complete chaos reigned before.

However, the main thing that dominates Reed throughout his/her life is the desire for some kind of growth, and most often; he or she devotes his/her life to making a professional career. If, for some reason, career growth becomes impossible (and as a rule, this happens in women), then he/she can begin to realize these aspirations in children. In general, in the depths of his/her soul, Reed always intuitively feels his/her closeness with children – after all, one sees in them the same desire for unbridled growth as in oneself.

In this attitude towards children, he /she often also do not know the measure, as in everything else.

The main feature of the Reed is that it enhances any of its features in a person – both good and not too good. That is why it is so important that Reed choose worthy goals for himself/herself in life and that his/her energy, which knows no barriers, be directed in a positive way. In this case, he or she has every chance to break through any concrete and asphalt and maybe even grow to the very stars.

Reed Man

According to the Mayan horoscope, the man of the Reed sign will certainly achieve his goal, even if it seems impossible: a leadership position, the heart of an impregnable beauty. For him, there are no obstacles and barriers, it is often too reckless, but his courage and determination are qualities that cause admiration. A man of this sign is not distinguished by constancy and strives to live in his pleasure. You can't rely on him; he often sacrifices the interests of close people. First of all, he thinks about his comfort. But it is never boring; he tries to color life with bright emotions.

Reed Woman

A charming woman of the sign Reed has a strong will and builds bold plans. In her dreams, she is a fatal woman, a successful business lady, a loving mother, and a faithful wife. Moreover, she talented embodies her ideas about the ideal life in reality. Her energy is enough for many things, but most of all, she loves to travel. Gives preference to work related to travel. According to the horoscope of compatibility, a calm, reliable man, ready for a serious relationship, suits her. For the sake of the chosen one, she can give up a successful career and fully devote himself to her family and children.

World Celebrities Born on Cane Day

Sigmund Freud (b. 05/06/1856) – Austrian doctor, psychoanalyst, founder of psychoanalysis.

Carl Jung (b. 07/26/1875) – Swiss psychoanalyst, student of Freud, and founder of analytical psychology.

Charles Dickens (b. 02/07/1812) – English classic writer.

Clifford Simak (b. 3.08.1904) – American science fiction writer, one of the most prolific authors in this genre.

Johann Brahms (b. 05/07/1833) – German composer.

Quentin Tarantino (b. 03/27/1963) – Cult American director and producer.

Justin Timberlake (b. 01/31/1981) – American singer, winner of the Grammy Award.

Mel Gibson (b. 01/03/1956) – Hollywood actor, director, and screenwriter.

Korney Chukovsky (b. 03/31/1882) – Russian children's writer, poet, and classic of Russian children's literature.

Girolamo Savonarola (b. 09/21/1452) – A fiery Italian preacher and social reformer.

Franklin D. Roosevelt (b. 01/30/1882) – 32nd President of the United States.

Erwin Schrödinger (b. 08/12/1887) – Austrian theoretical physicist, one of the founders of quantum mechanics.

Johannes Kepler (b. 12/27/1571) – German astronomer who discovered the laws of planetary motion.

Chapter 18 – Jaguar (Ix).

Name: I´X / Ix (Jaguar)
Meaning: Jaguar, Ocelot, Wizard
Element: Air
Direction: North
Compatibility: Jaguar, Flint, Wind, Scull, Dog

The meaning of the Mayan symbol

Those born on March 9, April 3, April 23, May 13, June 2, June 22, July 12, August 1, August 21, September 10, September 30, October 20, November 9, November 29, December 19, 8 January, January 28, February 17 in the Mayan Zodiac is called YISH (Jaguar).

Jaguar is the traditional name for this sign among the Mayan Quiche. In general, the Mayan Ix means "skin" and "emery."

On the hieroglyph of the Jaguar sign, in addition to the skin of the Jaguar, many grains of sand are also often depicted, and the dotted lines show the movement of sand during the grinding of the product, which expresses the idea of ending any business. The image of the jaguar, which was a cult animal among the Maya, symbolizes strength, determination, and intelligence.

In general, the sign of Ix, Jaguar, symbolizes such qualities as strength, will, determination, the ability to end things, and, most importantly, high intellectual abilities.

Jaguar character

Jaguar is a person who knows how to get his/her way. Nature generously endowed him/her with such traits as a sharp, observant mind, determination, and luck in achieving the goal.

Perhaps the main feature of a person born on the day of the Jaguar is his /her concreteness. He/she does not like vague wording; in his/her mouth, "yes" means "yes," and "no" always means "no." He/she has quite strong emotions; however, his thinking cannot be called emotional. He/she knows how to control feelings and has a very sober, practical mind. This person is surprisingly logical and consistent, and his or her judgments are always distinct and clear. Often these people do not need to study any business for a long time – they can grasp it on the fly and, most importantly, understand the essence and know how to put the knowledge they have gained into practice.

It is not surprising that three of the greatest geniuses in the history of humankind were born under the sign of the Jaguar: Leonardo da Vinci, Isaac Newton, and Rene Descartes. The unique accuracy of their judgments and the breadth of their interests distinguished all of them.

Of course, it is difficult to expect that everyone born on the day of the Jaguar will become a new Newton. Nevertheless, more than people of other signs, features such as logic and breadth of interests characterize each.

Jaguar person is distinguished by increased confidence in oneself and one's abilities; such confidence does not arise from scratch. Indeed, his or her ability to quickly draw reasonable and accurate conclusions gives him/her the right to have his or her own opinion on a wide variety of issues – even in those areas where he/she would seem to be not an expert. Such confidence attracts others to him or her and helps the Jaguar succeed in the cases he/she undertakes. No wonder the Mayans call this sign lucky.

The Jaguar knows how to do things and is used to bringing them to an end, an example of which is the life and work of the American entrepreneur Henry Ford born on this day. Until now, his name, which has become a world-famous automotive brand, is a symbol of American practicality and success. There is nothing superfluous in his cars, but they are distinguished by reliability, laconic beauty, and the best value for money.

Similarly, other Jaguars are good at organizing their affairs. They do not seek excessive luxury or convenience, are not afraid of hard work, and know how to firmly put their business on their feet, achieving success where others are ready to retreat ten times over. On this path, they greatly benefit from their innate practicality and concreteness, combined with a sharp mind and boundless self-confidence.

Due to his/her natural curiosity, the Jaguar is very receptive to everything new. He/she strives to keep up with the times and never looks old-fashioned. First of all, this refers to his/her increased interest in technical innovations and achievements since it is in technology that Jaguar sees the accuracy and practicality that he/she always strives for.

Such a love of the Jaguar for accuracy is also manifested in the fact that he/she physically cannot stand lies and deceit because a lie is a conscious distortion of reality that violates logic, and it is simply impossible for a Jaguar inclined to accuracy and concreteness to come to terms with this.

Another striking feature of the Jaguar is one's increased physical activity. He/she loves his/her body and likes to actively use it; his/her temperament does not accept passive rest. As a rule, Jaguars are very athletic, energetic people that are why they can find applications for their talents in business or science and sports. Moreover, they often manage to be realized in several areas! The most famous bodybuilder on the planet, Arnold Schwarzenegger, was born on the day of the Jaguar, while his passion for body culture did not prevent him from finding application for his sharp mind in politics as governor of the richest state in America – California.

However, it cannot be said that the Jaguar does not have any flaws at all. Due to his/her quick, concrete mind, his/her judgments are often characterized by increased sharpness and may seem categorical to others, even categorical. From the outside, the Jaguar can often give the impression of an imperious person who puts pressure on others – especially subordinates or their loved ones. Of course, he or she does not interfere with stroking this trait for a normal life, having learned to be more gentle and tolerant. But others should also remember that the peremptory nature of the Jaguar is most often no more than an illusion. It cannot be said that he/she does not listen to other people's opinions. On the contrary, he/she is always ready to curry favor with other people's arguments – but only if these arguments are justified, logical, and specific.

In general, the Jaguar (especially if he/she manages to balance his/her tendency to harshness and authoritarianism) is a very favorable sign for life and a career. This person is destined to live an interesting, eventful life, and his or her energy, sober, observant mind, and innate practicality will always help him/her take a truly worthy place in this world.

Jaguar male

According to the Maya horoscope, the man of the Jaguar sign is a leader in all spheres of life. He has no doubts about his superiority and considers it quite appropriate to distribute valuable instructions. Ready to accept someone else's point of view, but in rare cases, when the arguments cannot be refuted. Self-confidence and self-confidence are qualities that do not repel but, on the contrary, attract women to him. We are sure that a strong man is a worthy partner for marriage. However, he is too addicted, and you need to constantly think of ways to keep his attention.

Jaguar woman

The woman of the Jaguar sign is a beauty, a favorite of society. According to her love horoscope, she is destined for a happy fate. She has inner strength and magical abilities. Therefore, it easily wins the hearts of men. The side of trouble and sorrow bypasses the representative of this day; luck accompanies in all matters. But the flip side of her luck is fragile health. Unfortunately, she often gets sick, and tolerating even a mild cold is difficult. Therefore, she carefully monitors the state of her health and tries to do more sports.

World celebrities born on Jaguar Day.

Leonardo Da Vinci (b. 04/15/1452) – The greatest genius of the Renaissance.

Isaac Newton (b. 4.01.1643) – English scientist who laid the foundations of mathematical analysis and rational mechanics and also discovered the law of universal gravitation

Rene Descartes (b. 03/31/1596) – French philosopher, mathematician, physicist, and author of many discoveries in mathematics and natural sciences.

Ernest Hemingway (b. 07/21/1899) – American writer, Nobel laureate.

Ivan IV the Terrible (b. 25.08.1530) – The first Russian Tsar.

Margaret Thatcher (b. 10/13/1925) – "Iron Lady", the first female Prime Minister in the history of Great Britain.

Henry Ford (b. 07/30/1863) – American auto manufacturer, one of the founders of the global automotive industry.

Rudolf Diesel (b. 03/18/1858) – German engineer and inventor whose name is the diesel engine.

Benjamin Spock (b. 2.05.1903) – American pediatrician, Olympic champion in rowing.

Antonio Benders (b. 08/10/1960) – The first Spanish actor to be recognized in Hollywood.

Evander Holyfield (b. 10/19/1962) – The famous American boxer, the only 4-time world champion in the history of professional boxing.

Muhammad Ali (b. 01/17/1942) – American boxer, unsurpassed master of professional boxing.

Arnold Schwarzenegger (b. 07/30/1947) – A cult American film actor and politician.

Chapter 19 – Eagle (Men).

Name: TZ´IKIN / Men (Men).
Meaning: Opel, Bird.
Element: Water.
Direction: West.
Compatibility: Opel, Thunderstorm, Night, Deer, Monkey.

The meaning of the Mayan symbol

Those born on March 10, April 4, April 24, May 14, June 3, June 23, July 13, August 2, August 22, September 11, October 1, October 21, November 10, November 30, December 20, 9 January, January 29, February 18 in the Mayan Zodiac is called MEN (Eagle).

The Eagle is the conventional name for this Mayan sign – the Aztecs gave it such a name. Among the Maya-Kiche, it is called Tsikin, that is, "bird." As for the

Mayan name MEN, it means "business," "occupation," as well as "talent, ability."

The hieroglyph of the sign MEN usually depict an Eagle or human face, from the eyes of which a series of black dots extends towards the brain. In the language of the Mayan pictographs, this is read as "many-eyed" and "much-wise", meaning qualities such as observation and great intelligence. The hieroglyph at the top of the head often shows a straight horizontal line, which in pictograms usually means the highest level, the upper limit of something. In combination with much wisdom, this should be understood as an indication of maximum intellectual abilities.

Thus, the Eagle-Men – sign expresses the idea of the highest intellectual abilities.

Eagle character

A person who was born on the day of the Eagle is a born logician. It does not mean at all that he/she should be distinguished by a special quickness of mind, just that his/her mental potential is extremely high, and in any business, his/her logic prevails over feelings and emotions. Moreover, the Eagle person can often look slower than the others because one prefers to carefully think over the situation and only then decide. He/she does not like to rely on intuition and does not believe in instant insights, but, like no one else, he or she knows how to carefully and deeply analyze the situation before coming to any conclusion.

All this makes the character of the Eagle person quite balanced and calm. From an early age, he/she, as a rule, makes a very favorable impression on others – he/she does not like to argue, one is quite accommodating, and rarely comes into conflict, especially with parents and teachers (and in adulthood with his/her superiors), and also not only studies well, but also sincerely loves this process. Studying, unlike many other signs, is easy for him/her.

Often, the prudence inherent in the Eagle looks in the eyes of others as a sign of weakness or indecision. It is especially noticeable in adolescence when others demonstrate youthful recklessness and maximalism. However, it does not mean at all that the Eagle is weak-willed and ready to concede – it's just that, due to his/her intellect, he/she prefers not to go into a head-on collision but calmly looks for ways that will allow him or her to achieve the desired result with the least losses for oneself.

In other words, you should not think that if the Eagle gave in to someone's rough pressure, he/she thereby admitted his/her defeat. This impression is deceptive because, for him/her, a step back is just a tactic, but in fact, the Eagle will never back down from his/her interests and, at the first opportunity, will certainly do everything to turn the situation in his/her favor.

At the same time, others should consider that the Eagle person has an excellent memory and a cold mind. Retreating, he/she is not inclined to forget insults and forgive his or her offenders, and although he/she does not have such a trait as vindictiveness, any offense inflicted is an unresolved problem, and he/she does not like unresolved problems. It happens that even many years later, he/she returns to old conflicts with the sole purpose of showing his/her opponents that it was he/she who was the winner.

The Eagle person is very characteristic of such traits as pride and ambition. Often he or she needs not only to win but also to look like a winner.

In today's world, the Eagle is a very positive sign for life and career. Logic, sober prudence, and balance of people born on this day help them realize themselves in various fields – business, science, politics, and creativity. They have a sense of humor, they are not inclined to overdramatize the situation, they know how to show diplomatic flexibility, and at the same time, they have an amazing ability to search and find the best solution to their problems without unnecessary nerves.

However, Eagle's logic also has various weaknesses. Often he/she sins with excessive intellectuality, even abstruseness; paying little attention to the fact that his/her, reasoning is understandable only to a narrow circle of intellectuals like oneself.

In addition, the intellect of Eagle person helps him/her achieve his/her goals are also fraught with a catch. It happens that, intoxicated with success, the Eagle begins to believe in his or her omniscience and even omnipotence. In such a situation, he/she can easily indulge in all seriousness and make many sad mistakes. Alcohol, promiscuous sex, gambling – all this can imperceptibly drag the Eagle into its networks, which can be difficult to escape.

In addition, we should not forget that logic is far from one's only tool. In life, although infrequently, there are situations when the intellect is powerless. If a logical person finds oneself in a completely unfamiliar environment where he/she can rely only on intuition and instinct, one is simply lost. Such limitations of the intellect can manifest themselves in such matters as love, death, and indeed life itself. All these areas are incomprehensible to the logical mind, and if a problem touches them, the Eagle risks becoming confused and confused. In this case, his/her feeling of omnipotence can also be replaced by an awareness of helplessness.

Suppose the Eagle wants to overcome this limitation of his/her mind, inherent in him/her by Nature. In that case, he/she must first recognize that logic and intuition play a significant role in life. Without it, many discoveries, and indeed all-intellectual progress, would simply be impossible. Intuition is that second wing, having gained which the Eagle, with his/her wisdom, vigilance, and intelligence, can fly to the very heights, reaching unprecedented stellar heights.

Eagle man

In the Mayan calendar, Eagle is a sign of completeness and integrity. Therefore, the man of this day is a self-sufficient person. Maintains a reasonable balance between the physical and spiritual worlds but sometimes loses the ability to resist his personality's "dark" side. In this case, he becomes addicted to alcohol or starts numerous love relationships. According to the horoscope of compatibility, a faithful partner is suitable for him, possesses patience, and can make sacrifices for him. He is ready to devote himself to his chosen one but will not be content with a secondary role. He is a leader in love relationships.

Eagle Woman

According to the Maya horoscope, the woman of the Eagle sign is a mysterious person. She is endowed with qualities that are more inherent in men: iron willpower, firmness, and determination. Thanks to perseverance and determination, she consistently achieves success. Often, she is a famous person: a politician, a public figure. At the same time, the predator, by nature, knows how to create the impression of a feminine, fragile person. Talented manipulates the feelings and emotions of her partner. But often, she does not have enough patience or desire to bring the game to an end. She feels quite comfortable being in splendid isolation.

World celebrities born on Eagle Day

Blaise Pascal (b. 06/19/1623) – Famous French mathematician, physicist, religious philosopher, and writer.

Wilhelm Conrad Roentgen (b. 03/27/1845) – German physicist, discoverer of X-rays.

Jules Henri Poincare (b. 04/29/1854) – The great French mathematician who anticipated some of the Theory of Relativity provisions.

Marie Curie (b. 11/7/1867) – French scientist, Nobel Prize winner in chemistry.

Frederic Joliot-Curie (b. 03/19/1900) – French physicist who discovered artificial radioactivity.

Ada Lovelace (b. 12/10/1815) – English mathematician, the world's first programmer.

Emmanuel Swedenborg (b. 01/29/1688) – Swedish scientist and theosophist-mystic.

Woody Allen (b. 1.12.1935) – American intellectual film director, actor, screenwriter, and writer.

Winston Churchill (b. 11/30/1874) – British statesman, Prime Minister of England.

John F. Kennedy (b. 05/29/1917) – 35th President of the United States.

Chapter 20 – Vulture (Kib).

Name: AJMAC / Cib (Kib).
Meaning: Vulture, Owl, Bock.
Element: Fire.
Direction: South.
Compatibility: Vulture, Overlord, Grain, Sunrise, Ladder

The meaning of the Mayan symbol

Those born on March 11, April 5, April 25, May 15, June 4, June 24, July 14, August 3, August 23, September 12, October 2, October 22, November 11, December 1, December 21, 10 January, January 30, February 19 in the Mayan Zodiac is called KIIB (Vulture).

The Maya-Kiche and Aztecs call this sign a vulture, while the Mayan Kib means "wax", coming from the root "kib" – "cleaning." The bottom line is that the ancient

Mayans did not use wax at all, considering it to be waste. Subsequently, after European colonization, the Indians began to make candles from wax, the ancient meaning of the word "kib" was gradually forgotten, and it began to be used to refer to a wax candle. So, in the "Book of the Order of Days," it is said: "On the day of Kib, the Lord created the first candle, and light appeared where there was neither sun nor moon."

The hieroglyph of the sign Kib stylized depicts a honeycomb from which honey is squeezed out (the process of squeezing honey is depicted as a curved spiral in the center of the hieroglyph). In the figurative language of the Maya, this expresses a simple idea: to get to the useful, discarding everything superfluous.

Thus, the sign Kib, or Vulture, symbolizes clarity and purification in every sense of the word.

Vulture character

A vulture is a person with a sensual intellect. Nature endowed him with great mental abilities, but at the same time, dry, dispassionate reasoning is not characteristic of him. His/her feelings are so deep and strong that they inevitably leave an imprint on any of his/her thoughts. It can be said with certainty that a cool-headed analyst is not his style.

The depth of feelings inherent in Vulture person manifests in all possible areas of his life. On the one hand, by his/her very nature, one is disposed to sensual pleasures, loves to eat deliciously, and is not alien to earthly joys and bodily pleasures. On the other hand, it is very common for him/her to think deeply about moral and ethical problems. From a very early age, reflections on such concepts as good and evil, good and bad, and true and false are characteristic of Vulture person. In other words, Vulture person's intellect is not the intellect of a scientist cracker but rather a poet with a fiery heart.

Another striking feature of Vulture person's character is his/her tendency to directness, often perceived by others as excessive harshness of judgment. In a word, Vulture person does not suffer from an excess of diplomacy – rather, he/she suffers from a lack thereof.

Vultures often tend to be intolerant. They react very sharply to what, from their point of view, is wrong or unnecessary, but at the same time, they are not inclined to draw hasty conclusions, and even more so to judge anything indiscriminately. On the contrary, Nature has rewarded the Vultures with a very meticulous, corrosive mind. In everything, in every issue, they just need to get to the very essence, having analyzed the situation piece by piece. That is why Vulture person's opinion on all issues is very reasonable, and it is extremely difficult to challenge one.

In this sense, Vulture person has the qualities of a true researcher, and if it were not for his/her overly deep feelings, he/she could become an ideal scientist who knows how to find the very essence of things. Indeed, among famous people born on this day, there are many great minds. What is worth at least the name of the inventor of the first steam engine, James Watt!

However, due to their emotionality, Vultures more often choose for themselves the path of not a scientist but a poet, and there are many creative people among them. Such features as self-digging and the desire to understand their soul characterize them, and therefore very often in their life and work, there are themes of the struggle for justice and the search for truth.

In general, addressing moral issues is very characteristic of the Vulture person, but at the same time, hypocrisy, of which those around him/her are suspected, is not inherent in him/her. Of course, due to his/her high sensuality, Vulture person cannot live in a monastic way, and his/her behavior is far from always angelic, but the fact that he/she is sincerely capable of striving for moral purity is indisputable.

Interestingly, Vulture person's desire for purity can manifest itself even at the level of the body. In the depths of his/her soul, he/she often dislikes dirt in all its manifestations. Dirt irritates and turns him/her on. Sometimes this leads to the fact that he/she is ready to shower several times a day, feeling not clean enough. Such is one's nature.

Similarly, Vulture person can react to everything that, in his/her opinion, is superfluous or interfering. Among the Mayan Indians, the hieroglyph of this sign depicts the process of squeezing honey out of honeycombs, which expresses the desire of the Vulture to get to the very essence, getting rid of everything unnecessary.

Another manifestation of Vulture person's meticulousness and corrosiveness is expressed in the fact that he/she does not like to leave unresolved issues. He/she seeks to clarify any situation, any problem, by all means, having understood it to the end.

In everyday life, this often results in a showdown with others and, first of all, with loved ones. Such a feature of Vulture person can weigh on those close to him/her, but believe me, this is much better than hushing up problems and waiting for negative feelings to reach a boiling point. That is why in dealing with Vulture person, it is better not to avoid slippery moments but to calmly and soberly analyze the situation, coming to a joint decision. Believe me; Vulture person knows how to forgive. The only thing he/she will never agree to is to go against his/her ideas of justice.

Of course, the character of the Vulture can hardly be called simple and convenient for life. The reason for this is the increased depth of his/her feelings. Still, at the same time, Nature has endowed him/her with great inner strength, and the Vulture has every chance, having passed through thorns and discarding everything superfluous, to still get to sweet honey, having achieved considerable success in life.

Man Vulture

According to the Mayan horoscope, the man of the Vulture sign is strong, confident in his own right. He is able to make quick and, most importantly – the right decisions. People should respect his opinion and at least keep their doubts to themselves. He reacts too violently to criticism. He can flare up, say too much, and in rare cases, even hit. Therefore, in communication with the representative of this sign, it is wise to show calmness and endurance.

Vulture woman

The woman of the sign Vulture will not sacrifice her interests for the sake of a man. According to the compatibility horoscope, a strong, smart partner who knows how to make money suits her. But in personal relationships, the chosen one must yield to her wishes. Only in this case is a successful union possible. The woman of this day loves her children and takes care of them. She is often a mother of many children, but this does not mean she completely forgets about her interests. Personal hobbies for her always come first.

World celebrities born on the day of the Vulture
- **Arthur Clark** (b. 12/16/1917) – English writer, scientist, futurist,
- resident, etc.
- **Michael Douglas** (b. 09/25/1944) – American actor and producer.

- **Marlon Brando** (b. 04/03/1924) – American actor, roles in the movie "The Godfather", etc.
- **Bob Dylan** (b. 05/24/1941) – American singer and composer, star of the first magnitude in rock music.
- **Pablo Picasso** (b. 10/25/1881) – Spanish painter, author of the "Dove of Peace".
- **James Watt** (b. 01/19/1736) – An English scientist and inventor, invented the first heat engine, which essentially laid the foundation for machine production.

Norbert Wiener (b. 11/26/1894) – American mathematician, father of cybernetics.

Chapter 21 – Earthquake (Kaban).

Name: NOJ / Caban (Kaban)
Meaning: Earth, Earthquake, Movement
Element: Earth
Direction: East
Compatibility: Earthquake, World Tree, Grain, Water, Reed

The meaning of the Mayan symbol

Those born on March 12, April 6, April 26, May 16, June 5, June 25, July 15, August 4, August 24, September 13, October 3, October 23, November 12, December 2, December 22, 11 January, January 31, February 20 in the Mayan Zodiac is called Kaban (Earthquake).

Earthquake is one of the most controversial signs in terms of naming. In one's interpretation, the Maya always used a play on words. The fact is that in the Mayan language, the root "kab" means both "earth" and "honey," and therefore the word that is used in the meaning of "earthquake" can also be understood as "honey." Sometimes this sign is also called Incense.

Symbolically, this sign expresses the idea of sensual shock, overflowing with feelings.

The main element of the hieroglyph of this sign is a stylized image of a vessel from under the lid, of which a drop of honey flows. In this case, the vessel itself is usually depicted, as a graphic symbol of honey (a wavy curved line) and, at the same time, resembles the contour of a human face in profile. The vessel's lid (a straight horizontal line) in the language of Mayan images symbolizes the highest limit.

Most often, the hieroglyph of the Kaban sign also depicts a closed eye, to which a vertical row of black dots or strokes extends from below, which expresses the idea of gradual filling. The fact that the eye is closed indicates that we are discussing overflowing with thoughts, feelings, or fantasies.

In other words, the sign of the Earthquake is a symbol of strong feelings that overwhelm a person.

The nature of the Earthquake

A person born on the day of the Earthquake is a born dreamer and dreamer. He /she loves life and all earthly pleasures and is very partial to beautiful things, delicious food, good clothes, and pretty faces of the opposite sex, but here's the interesting thing: to be happy, he/she does not need to have all these things at all. The very consciousness that he/she theoretically can or could possess already fills him/her with a feeling close to euphoria. In other words, the dreams and fantasies themselves often satisfy the person of the Earthquake no worse, and it is often even better than their realization.

This is similar to how many women shop not to make a specific purchase but to "feed the eyes." People of the Earthquake often behave similarly, and in this, they are certainly right because they know the highest secret of the human soul: if you want to be happy, be happy.

You can have everything and not be happy, or you can be happy even without having almost anything – it all depends on the strength of the feelings that we experience, and in an Earthquake person, the strength of his/her sensations and fantasies is so great that it can satisfy him/her completely...

People of the Earthquake love to travel, and for this, they do not have to go to exotic countries. They are quite capable of getting full pleasure even from ordinary outdoor recreation. Here, too, they like to "feed their eyes" first of all, but they more than make up for the rest with their powerful imagination.

One could only envy such an ability of an Earthquake person to be happy in any circumstances, if not for one "but": an internally satisfied person loses many incentives to achieve a goal, and the fact that Earthquake people know how to be content with little often prevents them from achieving in life great heights. Indeed, why strive for the stars, even more wading through thorns, if it's so good? Instead, an Earthquake person can simply dream, having walked in a country park and getting no less, and maybe even more, pleasure from the simplest walk.

All this explains the strange fact that there are practically no those who would achieve fame in such areas as politics, sports, or business among the people of this sign. These people are dreamers, not fighters, and although it also happens that life elevates them to great heights, they rarely make great efforts to do so.

The best careers for people of the Earthquake develop if they find the use of their powerful imagination in creativity, where their emotionality and ability to enjoy simple things finds a use for themselves and can be very contagious. So, the great director Alfred Hitchcock, who was born on this day, did not raise super-complicated life topics in his films, but he knew how to enchant the viewer with the power of his completely indomitable fantasy, which had nothing to do with reality.

However, this sign has another downside. Just as people of the Earthquake, know how to sincerely rejoice in little things, so small troubles can sometimes hurt them too much, unsettle them and cause a whole storm of negative emotions. Another thing is that Nature has provided people with Earthquakes and protection from such unnecessary experiences: due to the same fantasy and dreaminess, they can simply "turn a blind eye" to troubles, switching their attention to something more attractive. And with their ability to find something pleasant everywhere, it is not difficult at all.

However, it must be taken into account that such a policy of "turning a blind eye" can only be effective when the troubles are minor. If the urgent problem is serious, then ignoring it can be simply dangerous. This can lead (and in most cases leads) to the fact that negative tension gradually accumulates inside a person, which eventually will surely break out, threatening to turn into a real explosion.

In this light, it becomes clear why the Maya called this day the Earthquake. Just as powerful tectonic energy imperceptibly accumulates in the depths of the Earth, which for the time being does not manifest itself in any way, but then suddenly breaks out, crushing entire cities, so for a person of this sign, avoiding a real solution to problems can turn into dire consequences.

This is the main paradox of the Earthquake: under its influence, people prefer not to notice obvious problems, they are easily carried away by fantastic ideas, not paying attention to reality, and in the end, and life itself reminds them (and often very painfully) that it is impossible to avoid problems. Fortunately, a person born on the day of the Earthquake is quite capable of doing this. In the Mayan book, *The Signs of the Days,* these people are called "very quick-witted". They have a mobile mind and are quite capable of solving their problems before they lead to dire consequences. Otherwise, the ability of these people to sincerely rejoice and enjoy the simplest things gives them every chance to live a long and, most importantly, happy life.

Man Earthquake

The Maya horoscope characterizes the man of the Earthquake sign as an energetic person full of life plans. Fountains with ideas know a huge number of interesting stories that he presents in his usual light manner of a joker and a merry fellow. Women love to be in the company of such a pleasant conversationalist. But family life with him is fraught with unpleasant surprises – novels on the side. A creatively gifted person does not strive for a successful career; the most important thing for him is inner feelings. He feels great to live the life of an ordinary employee.

Woman Earthquake

A beautiful, showy woman of the Earthquake sign is not deprived of the attention of men. Attracts the opposite sex with their sensuality and immediacy, causing a desire to protect and preserve. But she takes the smallest troubles too close to her heart and deeply experiences them. She tries to look calm and collected, but internal fears spill out in attacks of aggression towards loved ones. Fortunately, such behavior is rare. According to the Maya horoscope, a woman of this sign is lucky in all matters; she worthily passes her life path.

World Celebrities Born on the Day of the Earthquake

Alfred Hitchcock (b. 08/13/1899) – an Anglo-American director who combined the atmosphere of fear and irony in his films.

Antoine de Saint-Exupery (b. 06/29/1900) – French writer, philosopher, author of the books "The Little Prince", etc.

Arthur Hailey (b. 04/05/1920) – American writer.

Antonio Vivaldi (b. 03/04/1678) – Great Italian composer, virtuoso violinist.

Chris de Burgh (b. 10/15/1948) – Irish musician, singer, and composer.

Melanie Griffith (b. 08/09/1957) – American film actress.

Jackie Chan (b. 04/07/1954) – Popular Hollywood film actor and producer.

Demi Moore(b. 11/11/1962) – Hollywood star of the first magnitude.

Richard Gere (b. 08/31/1949) – Famous Hollywood actor.

Chapter 22 – Flint (Etz`nab).

Name: TIJAAX / Etz`nab (Etznab)
Meaning: Flint, Knife, Mirror
Element: Air
Direction: North
Compatibility: Flint, Dog, Wind, Scull, Jaguar

The meaning of the Mayan symbol

Those born on March 13, April 7, April 27, May 17, June 6, June 26, July 16, August 5, August 25, September 14, October 4, October 24, November 13, December 3, December 23, 12 January, February 1, February 21 in the Mayan Zodiac is called Etz`nab (Flint, Knife).

The Mayan Etz`nab means, "spear point," but it can also be understood as "sharp edge" or "splinter". Traditionally, this sign is interpreted as Flint since all the weapons of the Indians, including spearheads, were made mainly of Flint. Flint in Indian culture has about the same symbolic meaning as iron or steel. The Aztecs also put the same meaning into the meaning of this sign, calling it Tekpatl, that is, Flint.

The hieroglyph of the sign Etz`nab symbolically depicts a split stone in the form of two intersecting cracks. Sometimes a knife or a spearhead is depicted as a frame, but the main and invariable element of the hieroglyph is precisely the crack. This suggests that the main meaning of this sign is still not the flint itself but primarily its sharp fragment.

Thus, the sign of Etz`nab, or Flint, symbolizes strength, firmness, sharpness, and independence.

Character of Flint

The main thing distinguishing a person born on the day of Flint is his/her constant desire for independence and independence. Nature endowed these people with the strength of character and a powerful charge of self-confidence. They are fully characterized by such features as concreteness, clarity of thinking, and the habit of always and in everything relying only on their strength leads to the fact that in life, they, as a rule, can do a lot and often achieve significant success even without outside help. Thanks to this, many talented and bright personalities were born on the day of Flint, who left a deep mark.

In addition to all these qualities, a Flint man usually has great patience. If he has set a goal for himself, making him turn off the path is practically useless. Eventually, he will still achieve his goal and will not back down from his ideas. It's not that he is not afraid of difficulties and obstacles. He just tries not to pay attention to them, doing his job and arranging his life as he sees fit.

This approach can create many problems for Flint. He or she often lacks flexibility, and his/her words and actions often sin with straightforwardness. Such qualities as diplomacy and flattering politeness are not alien to him/her but most often unacceptable to him/her. Flint is better to remain silent than not to say what he or she thinks, although it can be very, very difficult for him/her to remain silent – they considers the most correct position in life to be telling the truth without hiding it behind ornate formulations.

However, not all this means at all that in communicating with others, Flint will always show harshness and rigidity. On the contrary, this person may appear calm, balanced, and even polite. Aggressiveness is not inherent at all. His/her principle boils down to a simple wording: "Do not touch – do not touch," but just try to put pressure on him/her or raise your voice, and one's sharp, tough answer will not be long in coming. At such moments, there may not be a trace left of Flint's endurance.

Flint is very characteristic of decisiveness – like no one else, he/she knows how to make decisions literally on the go. Such speed can manifest in the fact that Flint can suddenly quit the business he/she has begun if he considers it wrong or unnecessary, or he/she can no less quickly join some process. Others may perceive this as inconsistency, but the reason lies elsewhere: Flint simply needs to always and in everything precede from his/her convictions and principles, following which he or she chooses a line of behavior. Well, as for the main life principle of Flint, it comes down to a simple formula: "I decide everything myself."

In his/her decisions, these persons can even go against personal gain if they believe it will be better for business.

I must say that a main talent of Flint lies primarily in one's ability to achieve his/her goal – having chosen a goal, this person can be very stubborn and hardworking. He/she are observant and have a sharp mind, and, there is no concept of insurmountable obstacles, which is perfectly seen in the example of the Hollywood actor Bruce Lee, who was born on this day, whom Nature did not reward with either high growth or physical data. Who would have thought that this particular person, who looked like a frail teenager, would become a martial artist and the idol of millions of boys, proving the superiority of strength of character over any physical strength?

Another hallmark of Flint is his/her heightened sense of justice. As a rule, his/her aspiration of Flint runs like a red thread throughout his/her life, manifesting itself in all possible forms.

One of the most striking examples is the character of the great classic of world literature, Fyodor Dostoevsky, born on the day of Flint. This man went through a difficult path: in his youth, he participated in the revolutionary movement, for which he was sentenced to death, but literally, at the last second before the execution, he received a pardon. In all of Dostoevsky's books, the search for higher justice is the main theme – it is not for nothing that the most famous of all his works bears the telling title, *Crime and Punishment.*

Another question is that Flint's beliefs are far from always the ultimate truth, and this is precisely his/her main catch. Of course, firmness, determination, self-confidence, and the desire for truth can hardly be called negative qualities, but they are like sharp knives, which must be used carefully. After all, all people – including Flint – tend to make mistakes, but when this happens, decisiveness and confidence can turn into their reverse side. The Man of Flint is a fighter, which means that he/she, like no one else, needs to make the right choice for what and how he or she will fight.

If Flint learns to soften one's character prone to harshness, his/her undeniable talents and virtues will help him/her to achieve great heights in life. In this case, there will be no insurmountable obstacles in his/her way.

Flint Man

According to the Maya horoscope, the man of the Flint sign is a reliable protector. A brave and brave warrior can defend the honor of his beloved woman. With fearlessness, he rushes to solve her life problems. His energy is more than enough for both work and personal life. The only problem in communicating with him is intransigence. Natural stubbornness does not allow you to listen to the arguments of the mind and people's opinions. He rarely pushes even the most devoted fans away from him. According to the compatibility horoscope, a soft, indecisive woman suits him, who can truly appreciate love and care.

Flint Woman

In the eyes of the surrounding people, the woman of the Flint sign is a determined personality, adamant about her own, and even more so, about other people's weaknesses. She believes that every person deserving respect should have a strong character. She is not attracted to weak, insecure men. Strives to build strong relationships with a strong partner, although her unwillingness to give in often leads to family conflicts. The representative of this day should be more soft and feminine. Wisdom, patience, and restraint are the qualities necessary for a life full of peace and harmony.

World-famous people born on Flint Day
- **Napoleon I Bonaparte** (b. 08/15/1769) – The legendary French emperor and commander.
- **Fidel Castro** (b. 08/13/1926) – The permanent leader of the Cuban people until 2008
- **Lyndon Johnson** (b. 08/27/1908) – the 36th President of the United States, who started the war in Vietnam.
- **Nikola Tesla** (b. 07/10/1856) – Serbian and American physicist, engineer, and inventor.

- **Jules Verne** (b. 02/08/1828) – The famous French science fiction writer.
- **John Tolkien** (b. 01/3/1892) – English writer, philologist, and author of the famous trilogy "The Lord of the Rings".
- **Rudyard Kipling** (b. 12/30/1865) – English poet and writer.
- **Earle Stanley Gardner** (b. 07/17/1889) – American writer and author of detective stories about the lawyer Perry Mason.
- **Francis Coppola** (b. 04/07/1939) – Cult American director.
- **George Harrison** (b. 02/25/1943) – English rock musician, member of the "The Beatles" group.
- **Christopher Reeve** (b. 09/25/1952) – A cult Hollywood actor, the first performer in the role of Superman.
- **Keanu Reeves** (b. 09/2/1964) – Hollywood actor, leading roles in the films "The Matrix", etc.
- **Bruce Lee** (b. 11/27/1940) – Martial arts master, cult Hollywood actor.

Chapter 23 – Thunderstorm (Kawak).

Name: KAWOQ / Cauac (Kawak)
Meaning: Thunderstorm, Rain
Element: Water
Direction: West
Compatibility: Thunderstorm, Night, Deer, Master, Opel

The meaning of the Mayan symbol

Those born on March 14, April 8, April 28, May 18, June 7, June 27, July 17, August 6, August 26, September 15, October 5, October 25, November 14, December 4, December 24, 13 January, February 2, February 22 in the Mayan Zodiac is called KAWAK (Thunderstorm, Thunder).

The Mayan KAWAK is read as "to overturn, turn over," being a derivative of the verb "kaval"; however, traditionally, this sign is interpreted as Thunderstorm. This is connected both with the nature of the sign itself and with the play on words: "kawak" is consonant with the Mayan "k'a-vak'," which means "strong roar, crackling, or thunder."

The main element of the hieroglyph of the Kawak sign is an overturned hill consisting of separate circles. This slide is often limited from above by a straight horizontal line, which symbolizes the highest limit. The combination of the sign of the highest limit and an overturned slide should be understood as overcrowding and violent splashing over the edge. Another frequent element of the hieroglyph Kawak is an oblique cross, consisting of two short straight lines, meaning a crack, a split, or a breakthrough.

Often the hieroglyph of the Kawak sign is stylized as a human face in profile. At the same time, in place of the mouth, a grain icon (a rectangle divided in half) is often depicted, surrounded by many black dots. In the language of Mayan imagery, all this means a lot of talk and thoughts about wealth and abundance.

Thus, the Thunderstorm is a sign of overflowing with feelings, a sensual explosion.

Thunderstorm Character

People born on the day of the Thunderstorm share a very difficult fate. They react sharply to everything that happens, their nerves are always on edge, and although they get used to their constant nervous tension as a background that accompanies them all their lives, nevertheless, it often breaks out of them. On the other hand, so many celebrities who left behind such a bright, deep mark were born under no other sign. In this sense, the Thunderstorm is far superior to all other Mayan signs.

The Thunderstorm person is an extremely emotional nature. Even when outwardly he/she looks calm, in behavior, and especially in one's eyes, there is great strength in his/her feelings and inner tension. It is like a stormy sky, which can pour uncontrollable rain on the earth at any moment or be illuminated by lightning flashes. However, this applies to any feelings of the Thunderstorm – both positive and negative. At the same time, his/her feelings can change incredibly quickly. If they say that there is one step from love to hate, then the person of the Thunderstorm is not even a step, but half a step, so quickly he/she can move from stormy joy to stormy indignation, and vice versa.

However, not all this means that the people of the Thunderstorm in everyday life are completely uncontrollable. On the contrary, they are well aware of their deep emotionality and the possible consequences of this. As a rule, even from an early age, they are convinced from their own experience of the need to restrain their powerful, unbridled feelings and try their best to control themselves. Another thing is that with their temperament, it is far from always possible to restrain them, and their emotions still break out from time to time. Such is their nature, which they have no power to change.

Such a constant struggle with their powerful feelings tempers their will, making the character stubborn, but it also leaves an imprint of some kind of tragedy on them. Indeed, the eternal struggle with oneself does little to incline one to be a carefree, cheerful person. Therefore, much more often, people of the Thunderstorm have a serious expression on their faces – often with a touch of tension.

Even more, the character of the Thunderstorm is aggravated by such a trait as independence and self-will. With the strength of his/her emotions, he or she can simply not obey the circumstances or someone else's orders.

Of course, living next to such an independent person, whose feelings are so unpredictable and deep, is very difficult. The person of the Thunderstorm, one`s stormy character delivers many problems – his or her whole life is filled with powerful experiences and passions. On the other hand, in areas where the power of feelings is required, no one can match Thunderstorm person. It is very good when these people find themselves in art, where they can best realize their full potential.

In addition, due to their temperament, one often finds oneself at the epicenter of all kinds of scandals and bright events, which means that one`s chances of getting on the front pages of newspapers are as high as possible. Interestingly, the famous American journalist Joseph Pulitzer, who was born on the day of the Thunderstorm, is considered the father of the genre of the "yellow press," which feeds on scandals and scandalous rumors.

This is the main talent of the Thunderstorm person – to attract attention. To do this, he or she does not even have to be a participant in scandalous events: his/her extraordinary personality attracts attention. The secret lies in the fact that some kind of bewitching pre-storm power is read in their very appearance and eyes.

Not only emotions but also the very thinking of the Thunderstorm person is also distinguished by great strength and depth. Of course, he or she does not look like a scientist cracker, but on the other hand, he/she can bring his/her powerful inspiration and inspiration even to scientific creativity, coloring it with new bright colors. It is not surprising that many outstanding scientists were born under this sign. What are at least such names as Maxwell or Niles Bohr – one of the founders of quantum physics?

Another striking feature of the Thunderstorm person is indifference to wealth, fame, and, in general, all sorts of worldly temptations. Of course, dreams of fame and fortune are characteristic of everyone, but for no one else do these aspirations evoke such strong feelings. Moreover, the people of the Thunderstorm, as a rule, are disastrously unable to be satisfied with what they have. In this, they are characterized by the same excess and excess as in everything else.

In other words, the life of a person born on the day of the Thunderstorm person does not promise to be easy. It does not mean that tragic trials will certainly fall to his/

her lot – the main test of the Storm is oneself and his/her difficult character. He/she is like the energy of an atomic nucleus, which can be destructive, but can be curbed and channeled into a creative channel. Therefore, if a Thunderstorm person wants to live fully and happily, he/she needs to learn not so much to restrain him/her as to find peace of mind. Then the mighty force of his/her emotions will certainly turn into its positive side, lifting him/her to unprecedented heights – perhaps even inaccessible to anyone else.

Thunderstorm Man

The Man of the Thunderstorm sign is contradictory. Dreams of fame and recognition try to build a successful career. He suffers from fears and doubts. He feels a constant internal tension. In a love relationship, he seeks peace and understanding but often quarrels and cannot control his emotions. A man who can feel and empathize subtly can make an excellent pair for a soft, compliant woman. In a happy marriage, he can get rid of fears, worries, and find inner peace.

Thunderstorm Woman

The woman of the Thunderstorm sign is a bright personality that influences the minds of the people around her. A beautiful, fragile, gentle person excites the imagination of men. It seems that some kind of mystery is hidden in her. With a close acquaintance, she can manifest as an explosive, emotional person. According to the compatibility horoscope, a strong man is suitable for her, able to solve all her problems: difficult relationships with colleagues, poor health, and mood swings. With a worthy partner, she is ready to create a strong family. She will not seek adventure on the side. The woman of this day is a loving and faithful wife, a caring mother.

World Celebrities Born on Thunderstorm Day

Princess Diana (Diana Spencer) (b. 07/01/1961) – The infamous English princess who tragically died in 1997.

Yoko Ono (b. 02/18/1933) – Japanese singer, widow of John Lennon, who was widely accused of breaking up the Beatles.

Kurt Cobain (b. 02/20/1967) – American musician, vocalist, and guitarist of the cult band Nirvana.

Alla Pugacheva (b. 04/15/1949) – Russian popular singer, actress, and producer.

Jim Carrey (b. 01/17/1962) – American comedian actor, films "The Mask", "Ace Ventura", etc.

Nicole Kidman (b. 06/20/1967) – Hollywood movie star.

Brad Pitt (b. 12/18/1963) – A popular American actor.

Nicolas Cage (b. 01/07/1964) – A popular American actor.

Niels Bohr (b. 10/7/1885) – Danish physicist, creator of the theory of the atom, and one of the founders of quantum physics.

James Maxwell (b. 06/13/1831) – English physicist and creator of classical electrodynamics.

Maximilian Robespierre (b. 05/06/1758) – Figure of the French Revolution, organizer of mass terror.

Edgar Allan Poe (b. 01/19/1809) – American romantic writer and author of phantasmagoric short stories.

Joseph Pulitzer (b. 04/10/1847) – American publisher, journalist, and founder of the "yellow press" genre.

Chapter 24 – Lord (Ajaw).

Name: AJPUU / Ajaw (Axau)
Meaning: Sun, Flower, Lord of Light
Element: Fire
Direction: South
Compatibility: Grain, Sunrise, Ladder, Neck

The meaning of the Mayan symbol

Those born on March 15, April 9, April 29, May 19, June 8, June 28, July 18, August 7, August 27, September 16, October 6, October 26, November 15, December 5, December 25, 14 January, February 3, February 23 in the Mayan Zodiac is called Ajaw (Lord).

The Mayan Ajaw has the meaning "Lord" and translates as "the one who starts", "the one who distributes", and "the one who throws the enemy on his back" (from the polysemantic Mayan expression "ah-hau"). The Aztecs called this sign Xochitl, which means "flower of the day," the Sun. Sometimes you can also find another interpretation of its name: Ancestors.

The hieroglyph of the Ajaw sign depicts a stylized face of a shooter from a sarbakan blowpipe. The windpipe is depicted as a small circle inside a circle and symbolically expresses the idea of male power and fertility.

The main element of the hieroglyph Ajaw is two circles separated by a vertical double line. In the language of Mayan images, such a combination of symbols expresses the idea of dividing a crop or property (a circle means a part of something, and a double stripe means a division). In addition, the symmetry of the hieroglyph and division into equal parts express concepts such as "justice" and "balance".

In general, the sign of Ajaw, or the Lord, is a sign of power, balanced strength, and justice.

The character of the Lord

People born on the day of the Lord have the secret of incomprehensible magnetism. They are rarely alone, others are drawn to them, and companies occasionally form around them. Person of the Lord is characterized by such traits as self-confidence, cheerfulness, and sociability, which attract people to them.

At the same time, the Lord's inner balance does not imply passivity. On the contrary, this is a very active person with strong emotions, but he /she masterfully knows how to manipulate them. Nature rewarded one with a powerful reserve of active energy, thanks to which he /she can achieve very much.

Usually, the career of the Lord thrives. He /she feels good in leadership positions, knows how to organize an independent business, is not prone to unjustified risk, and rarely makes serious mistakes. Moreover, even having made a significant mistake, he /she can, as they say, get out of the water dry.

As a rule, such a feature as authoritarianism characterizes the Lord person; however, unlike many other signs, this quality is not striking and does not cause hostility. He /she can be very demanding, persistent, and even tough, but he or she knows how to do it carefully without causing active opposition.

This sign has an amazing talent for managing and organizing people around him/her. Often he/she does it so masterfully and imperceptibly that his or her organizational role is invisible, in full accordance with the ancient Chinese proverb: "The best ruler is not the one who is loved, but the one who is not noticed." It may seem to others that they make decisions themselves and act based on their interests, but in some incomprehensible way, the Lord person will always be in the center, and all events will revolve around him/her. It's just that Nature rewarded him/her with the talent to masterfully manipulate emotions – both his/her own and those of others. He/she intuitively, without even thinking, chooses exactly those words and that line of behavior that evoke the strongest feelings in those around him/her.

These feelings can be very different. Depending on the circumstances, the Lord person can inspire, resent, relieve tension with an unexpected word, and calm the emerging conflict. At the same time, he /she know how to move from one emotion to another so quickly that, as a rule, conflicts rarely arise in communication.

This is his/her talent as an organizer. His/her style is not to suppress emotions but to balance with others. With the same speed with which the Lord can cause discontent, he /she can, if necessary, reduce it to nothing, switching the interlocutor's attention. It happens that after a conflict, this sign resumes communication as if nothing had happened and, at the same time, behaves so sincerely that there is no trace of the former tension. Therefore, it is difficult to be angry with these people for a long time, and they, as a rule, are not offended for long.

However, this sign also has its downside. The fact is that not all emotions in life can be brought into balance, and when this happens, the Lord person risks losing control over the situation. Most often, this deficiency manifests itself in his/her attitude to health – his or her loved ones. Here his/her heightened emotionality can turn against him/her.

Of course, suspiciousness is characteristic of everyone in one way or another, but in the Lord person, this trait can reach the highest strength. Since he /she is not used to suppressing his /her feelings like others, then feeling worried about one's health (and sooner or later, it happens to everyone) and not finding a way to quickly improve the situation, he or she like no one else, runs the risk of panic. Here, this sign needs a doctor who will treat and calm him/her down, instilling faith in a speedy recovery.

In this regard, it is worth noting that Nature has awarded these people with colossal immunity and a strong, healthy body, which can only be envied so that if the Lord person is capable of seriously undermining his/her heroic health on something, then first of all, based on his/her suspiciousness and excessive experiences.

Another characteristic feature of the Lord person is his/her developed intellect. Surprisingly, for all his/her heightened emotionality, this sign usually manages to remain exceptionally sober, even prudent. He /she are very logical; strong emotions and feelings do not interfere with his thinking at all.

No wonder it was on the day of the Lord that the greatest genius of our time, Albert Einstein, was born, whose name has become a household name. It is simply impossible to call Einstein impassive – just remember his world-famous photograph, where the great scientist, not at all embarrassed, sticks out his tongue. Yes, and according to the memoirs of contemporaries, Einstein had an enviable sense of humor, knew how to put in place a well-aimed word, and was generally distinguished by the great strength of feelings, but despite such a temperament, few people managed to leave such a bright and significant mark on science.

In general, the sign of the Lord has a very powerful organizing effect on people – Nature itself has ordered that those around them be unconsciously drawn to them. This sign is a born organizer, and he /she has every chance to live a long, happy, successful life, especially if he /she manages to competently manage one's amazing abilities without wasting them on trifles.

Male Lord

The Mayan horoscope characterizes the man of the sign of the Lord as a person with a complex character. With all his radiance and openness, he is subject to bursts of rage, which he does not consider necessary to hide. He does not like to listen to criticism; he considers himself right in all situations. Longs for recognition and compliments sincerely rejoice in them. Moreover, it has a lot of virtues that deserve a high rating: kindness, honesty, and decency. He always keeps his word and fulfills his obligations but does not refuse the help of a loved one offered in a tactful form.

Woman Lord

The frivolous woman of the sign Lord seems to be the most cheerful and carefree creature on the entire planet. A bright, cheerful beauty excites the hearts of men. She likes to be at the center of attention. Loyal fans and faithful friends surround her. It is interesting to communicate with the representative of this sign; it is impossible to be offended by arrogant behavior. Therefore, other women love and appreciate her. According to the horoscope of compatibility, she will find happiness in an alliance with a strong, self-confident man who can put up with her little weaknesses: squandering and coquetry.

World celebrities born on the day of the Lord.

Albert Einstein (b. 03/14/1879) – The genius of the twentieth century. Theoretical physicist, author of The Theory of Relativity.

Alfred Nobel (b. 10/21/1833) – Swedish chemist, dynamite inventor, and Nobel Prize founder.

Vincent van Gogh (b. 03/30/1853) – An outstanding Dutch painter.

Victor Hugo (b. 26.02.1802) – French writer, a classic of world literature.

Hermann Hesse (b. 2.07.1877) – German writer and philosopher, Nobel laureate.

Erich Maria Remarque (b. 06/22/1898) – German writer, a classic of world literature.

Leonardo Di Caprio (b. 11/11/1974) – Hollywood star of the first magnitude.

Pope John Paul II (b. 18.5.1920) – One of the most popular pontiffs in history.

Conclusion.

In conclusion, the Mayan Horoscope offers a fascinating and unique perspective on astrology. Throughout this book, we have explored the rich traditions and beliefs of the ancient Mayan civilization, gaining valuable insights into their understanding of the cosmos and the role of astrology in their daily lives. The Mayans possessed an intricate and sophisticated system of astrology, which differed significantly from the Western zodiac we are more familiar with today.

As discussed in this book, one key aspect that sets the Mayan Horoscope apart is its deep connection to nature and the natural world. The Mayans believed that celestial bodies, such as the sun, moon, and planets, held great influence over human destiny. They understood the interconnectedness of all living beings and recognized the importance of harmonizing with the rhythms of the universe.

The Mayan Horoscope consists of 20 distinct day signs, each representing a different energy and personality trait. Combined with the 13 numbers, these signs create a 260-day sacred calendar known as the Tzolkin. The Tzolkin allows individuals to determine their unique birth combination and gain insights into their strengths, weaknesses, and life purpose. By understanding their Mayan birth sign, individuals can better comprehend themselves and their place in the world.

Throughout this book, we have examined each of the 20 Mayan day signs, delving into their meanings and characteristics. We have explored how these signs interact with the 13 numbers to create a complex and intricate system of personal astrology. Whether you are a Ch'en (Black Storm) or a B'atz' (Monkey), a K'an (Lizard) or an Ajmaq (Vulture), each day sign carries its own significance and offers valuable guidance for navigating life's challenges and embracing its opportunities.

To understand the Mayan Horoscope, you have to familiarize yourself with the 20-day signs that form the core of the horoscope. Each day sign represents a distinct energy or archetype, carrying its own traits and qualities. Explore the meanings behind these signs, their associated elements, and the animals or natural phenomena they symbolize. By recognizing your own day sign, you can gain valuable insights into your personality and life path.

Next, you must acquaint yourself with the 13 numbers accompanying the day signs. These numbers add depth and complexity to the interpretation of the Mayan Horoscope. Consider the significance of each number and how it interacts with your day sign. Understanding the interplay between numbers and day signs allows a more nuanced analysis of your traits and tendencies.

Additionally, you need to grasp the concept of the Tzolkin, the sacred Mayan calendar consisting of 260 days. This calendar combines the day signs and numbers to create a unique combination for each individual. Explore the Tzolkin and learn how to determine your personal birth combination. By understanding your specific place within this calendar, you can unlock a deeper grasp of your life purpose and the energies that influence you.

Lastly, recognize the cyclical nature of the Mayan Horoscope. Unlike linear concepts of time, the Mayans believed in recurring patterns and cycles. Observing these cycles allows you to discern broader trends and gain insight into the collective energies at play. This cyclical perspective enhances your understanding of both personal and societal events, providing a holistic view of life's ups and downs.

By immersing yourself in the Mayan Horoscope's symbolism, archetypes, numbers, and cycles, you can gradually develop a comprehensive understanding of this ancient astrological tradition. Embrace the wisdom of the Mayans and embark on a journey of self-discovery and insight through the Mayan Horoscope.

Mayan Horoscope places emphasis on cycles and patterns. The Mayans believed in the cyclical nature of time and saw it as a source of wisdom. They recognized that events and energies repeated themselves in predictable patterns, and by understanding these cycles, individuals could better prepare for what lay ahead. This perspective provides a refreshing alternative to the linear concept of time prevalent in Western astrology.

The Mayan Horoscope offers insight into individual personalities and life paths and provides guidance for collective energies and societal shifts. By examining the broader cycles and patterns within the Mayan calendar, we can better understand the world around us and the larger forces at play. This knowledge can be particularly valuable in times of change and uncertainty, helping us navigates the ebb and flow of life with greater wisdom and resilience.

The Mayan Horoscope presents a profound and illuminating system of astrology that offers a fresh perspective on our place in the Universe. By embracing the wisdom of the Mayan civilization, we can tap into a deeper understanding of ourselves, our relationships, and the world we inhabit. Mayan astrology invites us to reconnect with the natural rhythms of life, offering guidance and insight as we navigate our journey. So, let us embrace the rich tapestry of the Mayan Horoscope and embark on a path of self-discovery and enlightenment.

AUTHOR:

Olivia Stone

The Mayan Horoscope:
Ancient Secrets of the Mayan Calendar

Computer layout – L. Menchinskaya

The book was signed for printing on August 09, 2023,
in format 60 x 90 1/16.
Newsprint paper. Times type.
Conventional printed sheet 13,97. Circulation of 20,000 books.
Order No. 31-08. The price is negotiable.

Publishing house OVK.
04207, Kyiv, 5, Zoia Gaidai St.
tel. + 380 44 428 01 74, e-mail: office@owk.com.ua,
Website: http://owkbooks.com
(Certificate of inclusion of the subject of the publishing business in
State register of publishers, manufacturers, and distributors of
publishing products – series DK No. 4570 of 06/17/2013)

Printed in Great Britain
by Amazon